To those striving to keep our constitutional democracy—
and the rule of law—alive

Contents

Introduction

He'll sit here, and he'll say, "Do this! Do that!" And nothing will happen. Poor Ike—it won't be a bit like the Army. He'll find it very frustrating.

— President Harry Truman in 1952 considering the fate likely to befall candidate (and future president) General Dwight D. Eisenhower[1]

"Nobody knows the system better than me," Donald Trump proclaimed to the millions of viewers watching the 2016 Republican National Convention. He paused to elicit a reaction from the audience in Cleveland and smiled when the crowd cheerfully obliged. "Which is why *I alone can fix it!*" The audience roared its approval.[2]

Trump's campaign for the White House took the nation on a tumultuous ride. His campaign promises included the construction of a wall along the U.S.-Mexico border, a complete "shutdown" of Muslims entering the United States, a widespread dismantling of regulations, and the repeal of the Affordable Care Act, popularly known as Obamacare. A common thread running through these many promises was Trump's purported ability to get things done, all on his own. Yet on February 3, 2017—barely two weeks into his presidency—Trump ran headfirst into the formidable checks and balances that define our nation's constitutional structure.

That afternoon, President Trump's lawyers appeared before a federal judge named James Robart in a courtroom in Seattle, Washington. His lawyers were there to defend the legality of an order, issued by the president just one week earlier, that temporarily but immediately banned travelers from seven predominantly Muslim countries from entering the

United States. Trump's order had caused chaos at airports around the globe. Many travelers, midflight when the order was signed, were detained at U.S. airports. Others, unable to board their flights, were stranded at sites abroad. The media quickly spread images and stories of those affected: Iraqis who had served as interpreters for the U.S. military; a four-month-old Iranian baby with a heart defect who needed to travel to the United States for surgery; and more. Protestors responded by flooding airports across the country. Not surprisingly, legal challenges ensued.

One challenge, a lawsuit spearheaded by the State of Washington, was what brought President Trump's lawyers to Judge Robart's wood-paneled courtroom in Seattle.[3] The judge called the emergency hearing to help him decide whether to temporarily enjoin—meaning block—the president's travel ban. A no-nonsense Republican appointee sporting a black robe, a grandfatherly visage, and a striped bow tie, Judge Robart peppered both sides' lawyers with questions throughout the hearing. The judge listened carefully to their answers, then immediately announced his decision from the front of the packed courtroom. The State of Washington had demonstrated a substantial likelihood that the travel ban violated the law, he ruled.[4] As a result, the Trump Administration could no longer enforce the travel ban anywhere in the country, at least not without further judicial proceedings. Gasps filled the courtroom. Some observers wept with relief.

Back on the East Coast, President Trump forcefully questioned whether one federal judge in Seattle could singlehandedly put his travel ban on hold. He took to Twitter to object. "The opinion of this so-called judge, which essentially takes law-enforcement away from our country, is ridiculous and will be overturned!"[5] Trump's prediction radiated confidence. But it was wrong. An appellate court quickly issued a similar rebuke of Trump's order, and the travel restrictions remained on hold.

The on-the-ground effects of these legal developments were striking. Individuals across the globe who had been blocked from entering the United States were once again free to enter. Normal air travel resumed; families were reunited.

Yet this was not the end of the story for Trump's efforts to restrict travel. Instead, Trump withdrew his first travel ban and followed up with revised travel bans. Objectors, in turn, filed cases challenging the revised bans—and the federal courts, at least at the preliminary stages of these cases, also put the revised restrictions on hold. Amid this flurry of activity, these judicial rulings gave the president a very public lesson in civics: They confirmed that while the law does grant the president immense power, it also imposes significant limits. The president is not above the law.

Developments like these raise a seemingly endless series of questions about what exactly the law does, and does not, allow a president to do. This book offers answers. It explains the laws that govern presidential power by describing what the President of the United States can do, and how the president can do it. It also addresses the opposite set of questions, concerning what the president *cannot* do, and who has the legal power to stop him.*

As this book demonstrates, the U.S. Constitution makes it very difficult for any president to achieve significant change on his own. Although presidents throughout history have attempted to push through major reforms—with or without the support of others—these efforts frequently have failed. The obstacles to reform have come not only from the courts, but also from resistant members of Congress, cumbersome legal restrictions, recalcitrant states, dissatisfied voters, and other important forces. Occasionally, of course, presidents have succeeded in enacting dramatic change. Yet this tends to occur only when all the stars—political *and* legal—somehow align. Much more often, a president advances his agenda only incrementally, chipping away at initiatives that he disfavors and bolstering initiatives that he supports.

Like so many presidents before him, President Trump has seen his time in office fit this pattern. Take his first 100 days. During this time, the president was able to take important, but still limited, steps in advancing his political agenda. He successfully appointed Neil Gorsuch to the U.S. Supreme Court. He also signed resolutions passed by Congress that repealed more than a dozen Obama-era regulations, involving everything from guns to schools to the environment and more. The laws of presidential power allowed him to take these actions, and Trump

---

* Throughout this book, we exclusively use the male pronoun, rather than alternate pronouns, to refer to the President of the United States. While this practice tracks our historical discussions, it comes at the cost of more clearly acknowledging that Americans will, in all likelihood, eventually elect a female president.

seized the opportunity. Yet the first 100 days of Trump's presidency otherwise saw his major campaign promises, including the boldest of those contained in his "100-day action plan to Make America Great Again,"[6] remain largely unfulfilled.

What explains this disconnect? What explains the disparity between what some voters assume (or fear) a president will be able to do when he takes office and what he is actually able to accomplish? Politics, of course, play a major role. Just as importantly, *the law* through which politics operate provides critical context.

Exploring this law requires cutting through campaign promises and flashy headlines. It involves a journey through the text of the U.S. Constitution as well as the many other sources of authority that inform how the law empowers—and limits—the presidency. While the significance of these legal sources is complicated and often disputed, embarking on this journey is vital in a democracy. This is because effective civic participation requires understanding how the law works. Voters need to recognize what a president can and cannot do, as a legal matter, before they can put a candidate's campaign promises into context and more knowledgeably exercise their right to vote. Constituents need to understand how the law governs the president before they can assess the president's performance in office. Observers need to recognize how the legal pieces fit together to truly appreciate just how important *all* elections, not just presidential elections, are to a president's agenda. Perhaps most importantly, Americans need a working knowledge of the law in order to understand how best to support or resist the agenda of whoever is occupying the White House—both at this moment in history and in the future.

We begin our exploration of this law—the law of presidential power—at its foundation: with a description of our constitutional structure. As we will explain, the Constitution creates a system of checks and balances that divides power and prevents too much authority from falling into any one person's hands. We then turn to the powers that the law gives to the president. We describe where these legal powers come from and the key tools that presidents use to exercise them. This discussion helps to put into context what follows: an examination of the many participants, all empowered by law, who have the ability to push back against a president. These participants include Congress, the courts, others in the executive branch, the states, the media, and more. It very well may include you. To that end, this book concludes with ways you can participate in our government—and help to protect our democratic structures and the rule of law.

As authors, we have tried to limit our discussions to the law as it now stands. In other words, we do not focus on how understandings of the law have developed over time. This helps to explain why we primarily emphasize disputes affecting more recent presidents. We also refrain from opining on what we think the law *could* or *should* be. Rather, we describe the legal rules as they currently exist, including identifying where the law simply fails to provide clear answers.

In describing the law as it currently stands, we rely primarily on how it has been interpreted by the United States Supreme Court, as well as by the lower federal courts. This focus on the courts makes sense in light of the relatively stable tradition, among Americans, of accepting the judiciary's interpretation of the law as final and definitive. It also enables us, as authors, to draw on insights we both formed about the courts while serving as U.S. Supreme Court and appellate court law clerks, as lawyers working on behalf of clients, and as law professors. We recognize that this court-centered focus inevitably overlooks valuable interpretive work conducted by others. The absence of such analysis becomes particularly pronounced in certain areas, such as those involving matters of foreign affairs, where the courts may be unwilling to resolve disputes about the reaches of presidential power. In these spaces, the interpretive work of others, such as historians, legal scholars, and political actors, is particularly important. However, an examination of these other modes of analysis is another project for another day.

We also largely defer on the question of what might happen if the rule of law breaks down and a constitutional crisis erupts. This might occur, for example, if a president were to expressly refuse to obey court orders. Instead, we focus on what the law itself says about presidential power. In so doing, we describe how conflict—short of unresolvable constitutional crisis—is an inevitable part of our governmental system. Indeed, as we describe, the U.S. Constitution intentionally creates friction among the different branches of the federal government, as well as between the states and the federal government.[7]

In the end, what you will find is that our country's laws impose on the government a powerful system of checks and balances. The Constitution puts authority in "a President of the United States of America" to "hold his Office during the Term of four Years."[8] It does not put authority in a dictator. President Obama felt compelled to acknowledge as much in 2013, when he tried to explain delays in delivering on his campaign promises. A president is "not a king," he said. Rather, the president is "the head of the executive branch of government," and, as such, he is "required to follow the law."[9]

One consequence of these checks and balances is to give every person in the country the ability, at least on the margin, to help or to hinder a president's agenda. To that end, we conclude our book with suggestions for how to get involved. And we hope that you do. Our democracy may well depend on it—a reality that one of the country's founders, Benjamin Franklin, recognized from the very start. At the close of the 1787 Constitutional Convention, as Franklin was leaving Independence Hall, a woman asked him a question. "What have we got—a republic or a monarchy?"

Franklin gave her a candid reply. "A republic," he said, "if you can keep it."[10]

CHAPTER 1

Checks and Balances

Power must never be trusted without a check.

— Letter from John Adams to Thomas Jefferson in 1816[1]

The Founders of the United States preferred conflict over harmony. Under their logic, conflict inevitably arises whenever the law forces those in charge to share power. Conflict, in other words, is simply a sign of good government. The absence of conflict, by contrast, suggests a troubling accumulation of authority. And, as James Madison explained, the accumulation of political power is the "very definition of tyranny."[2]

Against this threat of tyranny, the Founders drafted a Constitution that slices up power and distributes it to many different governmental actors, each appointed or elected in different ways. As a result, no one actor in the United States government—not even the president—has an unchecked ability to make or revise the law.

For better or for worse, the divided nature of our government has stymied presidents throughout our country's history. For example, the Senate blocked our very first president, George Washington, from successfully appointing his preferred pick for a position in the navy. This resistance irritated Washington. Yet because the Constitution gives the Senate the legal authority to reject a president's nominees for certain high-level positions, he had no choice: Washington succumbed to the Senate's decision and nominated someone more to its liking.

Two centuries later, the checks and balances built into our constitutional structure continue to operate as powerful roadblocks. Take the presidency of George W. Bush. When Bush occupied the White House, he designated the privatization of social security as a top domestic priority. After his reelection in 2004, Bush threw his full weight behind this goal. "I earned capital in this campaign," he insisted. "And now I intend to spend it."[3] Yet Congress's statutes—not presidential fiat—govern our nation's social security system. And in response to Bush's entreaties, Congress refused to act. Without the support of legislators, Bush's privatization proposal remained just that: a mere proposal.

A similar pattern played out when President Barack Obama took office. Obama had campaigned on closing Guantánamo Bay, the American-run detention camp in Cuba. During his very first week in office, Obama signed an executive order instructing the government to shut down the camp "as soon as practicable," and no later than January 2010.[4] This instruction triggered fierce resistance from Congress, as well as from within the executive branch itself. What Obama's instruction did not do, however, was actually force the camp to close. Legal roadblocks—including statutes, enacted by Congress, prohibiting the transfer of Guantánamo Bay detainees to the United States—continually thwarted Obama's efforts. In the end, Obama was not able, even over the course of eight full years, to fulfill his campaign promise.

None of this is to say that the President of the United States lacks significant power. To the contrary, each president enjoys sweeping legal authority, especially in areas such as foreign affairs and direction over the nation's military. Indeed, if one considers the full range of the president's powers, it is hard to identify a single person in the United States with greater legal authority. All these powers nevertheless have real limits. Some of these limits are grounded in politics or other nonlegal forces, but many are grounded in law.

This chapter provides an overview of the legal divisions of authority that structure our nation's government. It begins with the U.S. Constitution, which sets the country's balance of power by creating a national government that divides authority among three branches: the legislative branch, the executive branch, and the judicial branch. In addition, the Constitution imposes separate divisions of power between the states and the national government. It then gives members of the public certain protections against the state governments, the federal government, or both. In other words, the Constitution does not concentrate power in one person, in one branch of government, or even in one government.

While these divisions of power make American governance more complicated than it otherwise would be, such complexity is crucial for maintaining what the U.S. Supreme Court has referred to as "a government of laws, and not of men."[5] This government of laws, in turn, requires that Americans work to understand—and to protect—its basic legal framework. As David Souter, a former U.S. Supreme Court justice, explained, if people do not understand how power is allocated in our country, they will not know whom to blame for the problems they are facing. This confusion might lead one person one day to "come forward and say, 'Give me total power, and I will solve this problem,'" Souter warned in 2012. "That is the way democracy dies. And ... that is what you should worry about at night."[6]

The Division of Power among the Three Branches

The Constitution divides the powers given to the national government (also referred to as the federal government) among three equal branches. A brief review of each branch helps to set the stage for the more complicated legal rules and debates that we will then explore.

First, the Constitution creates the legislative branch, consisting of the U.S. Senate and the U.S. House of Representatives. The Senate is made up of 100 members, two for each of the fifty states. Each senator is selected for a term of six years through an election that involves all of a state's voters. The Senate's relatively small size, along with its selection process (which shifted to a popular vote in the late nineteenth century), has contributed to the characterization of the body as "deliberative."[7]

Speaking to senators in 1805, Vice President Aaron Burr used over-the-top rhetoric to describe the Senate's strengths: "[The Senate] is a sanctuary; a citadel of law, of order, and of liberty; and it is here—it is here, in this exalted refuge; here, if anywhere, will resistance be made to the storms of political [frenzy] and the silent arts of corruption; and if the Constitution be destined ever to perish by the sacrilegious hands of the demagogue or the usurper, which God avert, its expiring agonies will be witnessed on this floor."[8] Burr's stirring oration drew some senators to tears. Hundreds of years later, senators still routinely suggest that the Senate does (or, at least, should) serve as "the world's greatest deliberative body."[9]

The House of Representatives is much larger than the Senate. Its 435 voting representatives are elected every two years in races that are not statewide but instead involve a geographically bound subset of each state's voters. (Exceptions come in states with very small populations, which have only one representative, who is elected statewide.) The number of members representing each state depends on the number of people living in that state. Populous California, for example, has over fifty representatives, while low-density Alaska has only one. As a result of these arrangements, the House is not only more sizable than the Senate; it is also more diverse and more frequently beholden to voting constituents. This tendency to track the political winds is by design. The Founders deemed it "essential to liberty" that the House of Representatives have "an immediate dependence on, and an intimate sympathy with, the people."[10] In this sense, the House helps to counterbalance more entrenched actors in government. Collectively, the 535 voting members of the Senate and the House must come together to make the laws that govern our nation.

The country's second branch is the executive branch, which is headed by the President of the United States. This massive branch is made up of more than 100 federal agencies (a number that fluctuates depending on how they are counted), including the Department of Labor, the Social Security Administration, the Department of Justice, and the Environmental Protection Agency. Each of these agencies was created, directly or indirectly, by Congress; none was established by the Constitution itself.

The executive branch employs more than two million people in its civilian ranks, with military personnel pushing that total to over four million. (By comparison, the legislative and judicial branches each employ around 30,000 individuals.[11]) The millions of people working in the executive branch help the president exercise what the Constitution calls the "executive Power,"[12] a power that includes carrying out and enforcing all the laws enacted by Congress.

The Constitution further empowers another elected official, the vice president, in a position that straddles the executive and legislative branches. The Constitution gives the vice president two main jobs. First, the vice president assumes the powers of the presidency if the president vacates his office, a scenario we discuss at more length in chapter 4. Second, the vice president serves as the president of the Senate, which means he is able to cast tie-breaking votes if the Senate is deadlocked. To the extent the vice president has other significant duties, they tend to derive from Congress or the president.[13] Congress has, for example, given the vice president a seat on the National Security Council, a council of high-ranking officers that advises the president on foreign affairs and national security issues.

The third and final branch is the judicial branch. It interprets the law in the course of deciding lawsuits that come before the courts. By constitutional design, the judicial branch consists of the U.S. Supreme Court, as well as other federal courts that Congress chooses to create. Congress has chosen to fill the judicial branch with two layers of federal courts below the Supreme Court: federal district courts, where most federal cases are first filed and adjudicated; and courts of appeals, where judges spend most of their time reviewing district court rulings. In the judicial hierarchy, federal district courts are at the bottom, the courts of appeals are in the middle, and the Supreme Court sits at the top. Yet even federal district courts possess tremendous power. For example, if a federal district court judge deems an executive branch action to be unlawful, that judge might issue an order purporting to halt the action nationwide, not just in the judge's own district. The ability to issue this sort of injunction is an extraordinary (and a highly debated) power. Yet unless or until another court overturns the district court's ruling, a nationwide injunction can block the executive branch's action across the entire country—as President Trump witnessed when Judge Robart enjoined his first travel ban.

Every single one of these judges—federal district court judges, courts of appeals judges, and Supreme Court justices—are appointed to the bench through a combination of the president's nomination and the Senate's confirmation. Once they are seated, however, the Constitution guarantees these judges lifetime tenure and salary safeguards. As a result, most of these judges will remain in office long after the end of the term of the president who nominated them. These constitutional protections are meant to insulate judges from political reprisal and, more generally, help the judicial branch operate as an independent branch of government.

According to the Founders, these divisions of authority—divisions that define our three branches of government—present a powerful defense against abuses of power. Abstract in theory but deeply consequential in practice, these divisions affect nearly everything that the United States government touches. As we will discuss in later chapters, they affect, for example, how federal officers and employees interact with the public, how laws are enforced, and how the country's resources are allocated.

Dividing Power between the State and National Governments

In addition to dividing power among the three branches of the federal government, the Constitution divides power between the federal government and the country's state governments. In this sense, as U.S. Supreme Court Justice Anthony Kennedy has explained, the nation's Founders "split the atom of sovereignty."[14] Indeed, "it was the genius of their idea that our citizens would have two political capacities, one state and one federal, each protected from incursion by the other."[15]

This innovative political arrangement—with two sets of governments governing in the same place, at the same time, with neither entirely in charge of the other—produces what is called a federation. In the United States, our federation includes fifty separate state governments, each with control over its own affairs. Describing these state governments in general terms can be difficult, given that each has unique features. Yet all have adopted governments consisting of the same three branches of government (legislative, executive, and judicial), albeit in different forms. Each state has a governor, rather than a president, and each has structured its legislative branch in its own way. For example, most states have two legislative bodies, loosely analogous to the U.S. House of Representatives and Senate, while Nebraska has only one. Each state also has its own court system and individually decides how its state court judges will be selected and whether they will enjoy job protections.

In allocating power among the state and national governments, the U.S. Constitution does not make the national government all-powerful. To the contrary, the Constitution gives the national government only limited powers, and it expressly provides that all powers *not* given to the national government are reserved to the states, or to the people within those states.[16] This distribution of power among these sovereign governments (state and federal) is often referred to as federalism.

Fierce debates over questions of federalism have erupted throughout the country's history. We will explore this complex relationship between the national and state governments in more detail in chapter 7. For now, three overarching principles are helpful to keep in mind.

First, the Constitution says that whenever there is a conflict between a federal law and a state law, the federal law wins.[17] Assume, for example, that a federal statute requires certain drugs to be packaged with an all-blue label. A state statute requires that those same drugs be packaged with an all-red label. It would be impossible for a drug packager to comply with both laws at once. The laws are therefore in conflict, and the U.S. Constitution requires that the state law yield.[18] (In other words, those labels are going to be blue.) These sorts of state-federal legal conflicts arise with some frequency. Still, if there is no conflict between the state and federal laws, the state law normally remains valid and controlling.[19]

Second, state governments tend to impose a lot of rules within their own borders. This is particularly true in areas where the federal government has not regulated very heavily, where the federal government lacks the legal power to regulate, or where the federal government has failed to address a problem that the states view as important. For example, as we will explore in more detail in chapter 9, many states have passed laws to combat climate change in an attempt to compensate for the federal government's relative lack of action at the national level. More generally, state governments tend to set most of the laws relating to, among other things, family issues (such as marriage, divorce, and custodial matters), criminal prohibitions, property rights, and contracts.

Third, because states are their own sovereign governments, they can choose to support or push back against the national government, including the president. A state that wants to cooperate with a president can offer the services of its state employees to help the president with his preferred projects. A state that wants to resist the president can refuse to provide such assistance.

States, in short, have a great deal of power in our constitutional system. As a result, state governments have a special ability to help, or hinder, a president's agenda.

The People's Rights

Having divided power horizontally and vertically, the Constitution makes one more set of critical divisions: It grants individuals a set of rights that the government may not infringe. In other words, the Constitution recognizes that certain individual rights are so important that they must be placed "beyond the reach of majorities and officials" and cannot be violated by the government, even if politicians (or their voting constituents) want them to be.[20]

The First Amendment, for example, prohibits the federal and state governments from violating individuals' free-speech rights. This same amendment also protects each person's right to engage in religious exercise, and it prohibits the government from establishing a national religion. Another important constitutional protection, contained in the Due Process Clauses of the Fifth and Fourteenth Amendments, prohibits the government from taking away a person's "life, liberty, or property" (as the courts have defined those terms) without first providing adequate procedures and justifications.

The legal scope and operation of each of these individual rights is complicated and disputed. What remains clear, however, is that these rights are highly relevant to the structure of the United States government, and more specifically to the scope of presidential power. This is because these rights serve as yet another limit on what the government can do. When any member of the government—including the president—acts in a manner that violates these rights, then normally that action cannot stand. This limitation on the government's powers helps to explain, for example, why several federal courts put President Trump's first travel ban on hold in early 2017. Those courts had concluded that the president's order likely violated individuals' rights.

In Sum: The Constitution Divides Power to Prevent Tyranny

In the hierarchy of the United States government, no one sits at the very top. Not even the president. Instead, many different actors—all governed by the rule of law—jostle for control within a complicated system of divided government.

This complexity is by design. Instead of consolidating power in one person's hands, the Constitution carefully divides authority among three branches of the federal government, and it empowers each branch to check and balance the others. The Constitution also divides power among the federal government and the fifty state governments, with the state and federal governments all operating independently. The Constitution divides power still further by protecting individual members of the public against certain types of encroachments by governmental entities and actors. As a consequence of these complicated divisions of authority, it is very difficult for any one person—even the president—to dictate how the law will be applied, to aggressively push through reforms, or otherwise to accomplish much without the support of others.

Undoubtedly, the president wields significant power. Yet this is not because the laws provide no check. Rather, it is because the laws are what empower the president—and with those laws come limits.

CHAPTER 2

The President's Powers

The President's power, if any, to issue the order must stem either from an act of Congress or from the Constitution itself.

— Justice Hugo Black writing for the U.S. Supreme Court in 1952 in *Youngstown Sheet & Tube Company v. Sawyer*[1]

The early 1950s saw the United States locked in protracted conflict with North Korea. Out of these hostilities emerged a legal dispute turning on the limits of presidential authority. Called to resolve the controversy, the Supreme Court responded with what might be the most important ruling it has ever issued on the scope of a president's powers.[2]

The drama began with the Korean War, which had devolved into an expensive and destructive stalemate. American bombers had been leveling cities and killing thousands, and they continued to bombard North Korea with explosives. Yet no resolution to the war was in sight. As a result, American military forces needed a functioning supply chain. For President Harry S. Truman, that meant steel.

Back in the United States, unfortunately, labor strife threatened steel production. The steelworkers union warned that its members would strike unless they received a wage increase. Yet without an agreement by the government to raise the price of steel, management refused to increase steelworkers' pay. Fearful that a strike could lead to a steel shortage and hurt the military effort, Truman encouraged the union and the companies to work out their disagreements. The president's outreach failed. So in April 1952—just hours before the steelworkers were set to strike—Truman took matters into his own hands. He ordered government officials to seize control of the nation's private steel mills and operate them without the owners' consent. This audacious seizure of private property was necessary, Truman insisted, because the nation's military strength depended on a "continuing and uninterrupted supply of steel."[3]

In response, the steel mill companies turned to their lawyers, who took less than an hour to find a federal judge and demand that the judge block Truman's order.[4] The companies' objections led to a flurry of litigation, culminating in *Youngstown Sheet & Tube Company v. Sawyer*, a landmark decision addressing the legal limits of the president's powers. In that case, the U.S. Supreme Court made clear that Truman had overstepped his bounds. Why? Because "the President's power, if any, to issue the order must stem either from an act of Congress or from the Constitution itself."[5] According to the court, neither the Constitution nor a law passed by Congress had given the president the power to take possession of private steel mills. As a result, the *Youngstown* ruling returned control of the mills to their owners. It also sent the president a clear message: Presidential power has limits—and the law defines those limits.

However sliced, the law governing presidential power is complicated and endlessly disputed. Even Justice Robert Jackson, who served as attorney general under President Franklin D. Roosevelt before joining the U.S. Supreme Court, bemoaned the lack of clarity surrounding presidential power. "A judge, like an executive adviser, may be surprised at the poverty of really useful and unambiguous authority applicable to concrete problems of executive power as they actually present themselves," he wrote while considering the claims in *Youngstown*.[6]

Still, it is clear that the president's powers are grounded in at least two sources: the Constitution and laws passed by Congress.[7] The Constitution itself provides the president with a range of powers, including the power to veto bills passed by Congress and act as the nation's commander in chief. Layered on top of these important constitutional grants of authority are various laws passed by Congress. These congressionally enacted statutes grant the president and members of the executive branch even more power, including the authority to carry out policies that touch nearly all aspects of people's lives: from food safety to drug packaging to tax liabilities to health insurance.

All these sources of law, whether constitutional or statutory, combine to give the president vast and far-reaching powers. Still, as President Truman learned from the *Youngstown* case—and as Trump learned when the courts blocked his first travel ban order—the president's powers are far from limitless.

What the Constitution Says about Presidential Power

The Constitution creates the office of the presidency. Yet it has relatively little to say about the scope of the powers held by its occupant. The short list of powers that the Constitution expressly grants to the president includes the power to:

- Propose laws to Congress;
- Veto or sign bills passed by both houses of Congress;
- Appoint Supreme Court justices and other key government officers (subject to approval by the Senate);
- "Take Care that the Laws be faithfully executed";[8]
- Act as the commander in chief of the military; and
- Make treaties with foreign countries (also subject to approval by the Senate).

Add a few more items to the list (such as the duty to deliver the State of the Union address and the authority to pardon crimes), and there you have the entirety of what the text of the Constitution says about presidential powers.

Despite the brevity of this list, the Constitution plays such a central role in setting our government's balance of power that any legal analysis of the president's powers must begin here. Each of the powers that the Constitution grants to the president—some set forth in its explicit text, others implied from its language and structure—can be identified and explored. Collectively, they give the president a great deal of authority.

The Power to Recommend and Veto (but Not Make) Law

The Constitution expressly gives Congress, not the president, the power to make law.[9] Truman received that reminder from the Supreme Court in

Youngstown. Nevertheless, the Constitution does give the president two express powers that enable him to influence the legislative process.

First, the Constitution empowers the president to recommend laws to Congress that he deems "necessary and expedient."[10] What the Constitution does not do is require Congress to accept what the president recommends. In 1993, for example, President Bill Clinton delivered to Congress a 240,000-word legislative blueprint for the adoption of universal health insurance.[11] Too few members of Congress were willing to go along with the plan, however, and the president's proposal never became law.

Still, at least as a political matter, this constitutionally conferred authority may help a president persuade Congress to enact major legislative reform. The Civil Rights Act of 1964 provides an important example. On entering the White House in 1961, President John F. Kennedy intended to wait until later in his presidency, perhaps even after reelection, before proposing legislation that would displace the South's segregationist Jim Crow laws. Yet events in the nation made waiting feel impossible. From sit-ins at lunch counters to Freedom Rides on buses, the cries for equality grew louder and louder. Then, in 1963, the news media shocked the nation with images of police officers in Alabama using dogs and high-pressure water hoses against black demonstrators, including students and children. These events convinced Kennedy that the government could no longer ignore the mounting calls for action. So, in June 1963, he announced to the nation in a televised address that he was asking Congress to pass civil rights legislation. The country was facing a "moral crisis," he argued, and it could not be "left to increased demonstrations in the streets" or "token moves or talk."[12] Rather, the crisis called for a legislative response. Soon after, Kennedy delivered a detailed civil rights bill to Congress.

When Kennedy was assassinated later that year, President Lyndon B. Johnson picked up where Kennedy left off, working over the span of many months to push the Civil Rights Act through Congress. Johnson used his high-profile status as president to aggressively prod, coerce, and bargain with specific members of Congress. In so doing, he relied on what is often called the president's "power to persuade."[13] Eventually this political persuasion paid off, and the bill became law. Today the Civil

Rights Act stands as one of the nation's landmark accomplishments in the field of civil rights.

In addition to giving the president the power to recommend laws to Congress, the Constitution also allows him to veto—meaning block—the passage of laws.[14] Through this veto power, the president can forcefully push back on Congress's agenda. President George Washington exercised the very first presidential veto, back in 1792, when he blocked a bill that would have affected the composition of the U.S. House of Representatives. A more modern example includes President Nixon's 1971 veto of a bill that would have implemented a system of universal, federally financed day care. An even more recent example came in 2016, when President Obama vetoed a bill that sought to repeal his signature health-care legislation. Over time, presidents have vetoed more than 2,500 bills passed by Congress. President Franklin D. Roosevelt holds the high score, with a whopping 635 vetoes.[15]

When Congress presents a bill to the president for his consideration, the president must either agree to the whole bill passed by both houses of Congress, allowing it all to become law, or veto the whole thing. He cannot sign most of a bill into law but make a few tweaks or line edits.[16] Given that a president sometimes supports only part of a bill, this all-or-nothing choice can put him in a difficult position. In response, a president occasionally will issue a written statement when signing a bill into law. This signing statement sets forth the president's views (whether negative or positive) about the bill, and it might include his thoughts about whether the law is constitutional or how the law should be interpreted. Yet even a signing statement does not allow a president to edit or otherwise change the text of the bill that Congress presents to him.[17]

If the president chooses to veto a bill instead of signing it into law, he usually returns the whole bill to Congress with a message explaining his reasoning. President Grover Cleveland did as much in 1887, for example, when he criticized the idea of government aid in explaining his veto of the Texas Seed Bill. In that bill, Congress proposed to provide $10,000—about $250,000 in today's dollars—to purchase seeds for farmers in Texas after a serious drought ruined their crops. The amount was relatively small, and the farmers' misfortune quite significant. Yet the president was not swayed.[18]

"Government should not support the people," Cleveland explained in his veto message.[19] "Federal aid in such cases encourages the expectation of paternal care on the part of the Government and weakens the sturdiness of our national character."[20] Legally speaking, at least, Cleveland's justification was more than sufficient. The Constitution does not impose any substantive requirements at all regarding the explanations that presidents provide when vetoing bills.

Even after a bill has been vetoed, Congress can enact it into law with a two-thirds majority of both houses of Congress.[21] The trouble is, to quote one scholar, "two-thirds of the members of both houses would fail to agree on the proposition that the marigold is a pretty flower."[22] Tellingly, even the proponents of the politically popular Texas Seed Bill failed to convince enough members of Congress to override Cleveland's veto.[23]

In short, the veto power is a politically important, and legally straightforward, source of power for a president.

The Power to Appoint Officers and Judges

A somewhat more complicated power that the Constitution gives to the president involves the authority to appoint high-ranking government officials and federal judges. Specifically, the Constitution gives the president the power, subject to the "Advice and Consent of the Senate," to appoint high-ranking government officials to help him execute the law, as well as federal judges who interpret the law.[24] In addition, the Constitution empowers Congress, if it so chooses, to enact statutes that give the president the power to appoint certain lower-level (but still quite high-ranking) officials all on his own, without any need for the president to seek Senate approval.[25]

The president's power over appointments is significant. At the outset, the appointment power gives the president an opportunity to shape the federal courts by nominating jurists whose views of the law are consistent with his own—a topic we will discuss in more detail in chapter 6.

In addition, the appointment power also enables the president to handpick officials, whom the Constitution refers to as "officers," to fill the highest ranks of the executive branch.[26] As of 2017, the president has the power to appoint approximately 1,200 high-ranking government officers with the Senate's consent. These officers help to run different agencies and departments, such as the Environmental Protection Agency, the Department of Justice, the Department of Homeland Security, and the State Department. Within the Department of Justice alone, for example, the president has the authority, subject to the Senate's approval, to select not only the attorney general but also more than 200 other high-ranking officials, including the heads of the Federal Bureau of Investigation and the Drug Enforcement Administration.[27] Given the role that these officials play in helping the president execute the laws—a separate power we soon will discuss—the president's power of appointment gives him significant leverage in advancing his political agenda.

The Power to Remove Officers (but Not Judges)

At least as important as the ability to hire key government officials is the authority to fire them. In this respect, however, the Constitution gives the president a mixed set of powers.

First, with respect to the judicial branch, the Constitution gives the president no ability, in any circumstance, to remove a judge from office. Instead, federal judges can be removed from office only if they are impeached by the House and convicted by the Senate—something that rarely occurs.[28] Tellingly, only eight judges have ever been impeached and convicted and thereby removed. The first was John Pickering, who was removed in 1804 on charges of lawlessly mishandling a case and other offenses. One article of impeachment accused him of "being a man of loose morals and intemperate habits."[29] A judge more recently removed was Alcee Hastings, who was forced out in 1989 for perjury and conspiring to solicit a bribe. Since that time, remarkably, Hastings has served more than twenty-five years as a representative in Congress from Florida.

Judges like Pickering and Hastings are the exceptions. Since the founding of the country, more than 3,000 judges have been appointed to the federal judiciary but never removed. In addition, no justice has ever been removed from the U.S. Supreme Court. As this history confirms, those appointed to the federal bench have powerful protections against political reprisal. It is extraordinarily difficult to fire them—and the power to accomplish this rare feat rests with Congress, not the president.

By contrast, when it comes to the tenure of executive branch officers, the president has much more power. According to the Supreme Court, the Constitution requires that the president have significant authority to fire officers who help the president execute the law. This means that a president often can fire high-ranking executive officers for almost any reason at all. "Without such power," Chief Justice John Roberts explained in 2010, "the President could not be held fully accountable for discharging his own responsibilities; the buck would stop somewhere else."[30]

Still, the president's authority to remove officers is not without legal limit. If Congress wants to limit the president's removal power, it can do so in certain circumstances by passing a statute. For example, in passing the statute that created the Federal Trade Commission (FTC), Congress limited the president's ability to fire the commission's highest-ranking officers. Specifically, Congress provided that the president can fire FTC commissioners only for "inefficiency, neglect of duty, or malfeasance in office."[31] In 1935, the Supreme Court concluded that this limitation was a constitutionally permissible restriction on the president's removal powers.[32]

Congress tends to impose these sorts of limits on removal when it wants to protect high-level officials from a president's influence.[33] In light of this, agencies run by officials with congressionally conferred protections against removal are frequently referred to as "independent agencies." The FTC is one example of an independent agency.

Often, however, Congress chooses not to restrict the president's ability to fire high-level officials. With respect to these officials, the president generally can exercise his default authority—meaning that he can fire these officers for almost any reason, even due to simple policy disagreements. From the head of the Environmental Protection Agency to the head of the Department of Justice, these executive officers hold their positions only so long as the president wants them in office.

These constitutionally grounded legal principles help to explain why, for example, President Trump was able to fire Sally Yates, a near-thirty-year veteran of the Department of Justice, just ten days after he took office. Yates had been serving as acting attorney general, which at the time was the nation's top law-enforcement officer. In this role, she was responsible for defending Trump's first travel ban against legal challenges.

Yet in a remarkable announcement issued on January 30, 2017, Yates explained that she would not stand behind the president's order.

"I am responsible for ensuring that the positions we take in court remain consistent with this institution's solemn obligation to always seek justice and stand for what is right," she announced.[34] "For as long as I am the Acting Attorney General, the Department of Justice will not present arguments in defense of the executive order."[35]

Trump's administration, still in its infancy, understood this as a crisis. And so, within hours of Yates's announcement, President Trump fired her for insubordination. Given that the attorney general works at the pleasure of the president, this firing was well within the president's legal authority.

Things became more complicated in May 2017 when President Trump fired James Comey, the director of the FBI. Initial reports from the White House suggested that it was Comey's 2016 handling of a prior investigation that had motivated Trump to fire him. Taken at face value, these reports meant that the termination likely was legal, just as it was when Trump fired Sally Yates. Congress had not placed any express restrictions on the president's ability to fire the FBI director, and so the president had wide latitude in making the decision to terminate. The trouble for Trump, according to the prevailing legal consensus, was that a president may not use his removal power—or, indeed, any of his powers—to commit a crime.[36] And after Trump fired Comey, accusations of criminal activity began to fly.

More specifically, critics of Trump argued that Comey had actually been fired because the president wanted to stop the FBI from conducting an ongoing investigation—including into allegations that members of Trump's campaign team had illegally conspired with Russian agents to influence the 2016 presidential election. If Trump had fired Comey for this reason, then, according to some legal experts, Trump might have violated criminal prohibitions against obstructing justice.[37]

Still, as this discussion reveals, the job security of many high-ranking officers, like the FBI director and the attorney general, primarily depends on the president's preferences and whims. While Congress does have some power to limit the president's removal power over these officials by enacting statutes, it often chooses not to impose these limits. The removal authority that remains with the president is significant because, as we will discuss in chapter 3, the president can use his leverage and influence over these high-ranking executive branch officials to advance his own political ends.

The Power to Execute the Law

Closely related to the president's power to appoint and remove officers is the president's power to execute the nation's laws. Specifically, the Constitution provides that the "executive Power shall be vested in a President of the United States," and it states that the president shall "take Care that the Laws be faithfully executed."[38] At its core, this grant of authority makes the president, aided by those officers who work underneath him within the executive branch, responsible for implementing and enforcing the nation's many laws. These laws govern everything from the quality of the nation's air to social security benefits, from drug laws to the safety of toys.

Take, for example, a law passed by Congress that protects employees in the labor market, including children who work as employees.[39] To carry out this law, individuals within the executive branch need to determine which employees and employers are covered by the statute, and what to do if an employer violates the law. To assist with this process, members of the executive branch, including those at the Department of Labor, interpret the statute and enact regulations to resolve any ambiguities in the law. For example, the congressional statute expressly exempts certain employees from some of the law's protections: namely, employees, including children, who are "engaged in the delivery of newspapers to the consumer."[40] (Think of the job performed by those historically referred to as paperboys.) But what about employees who, rather than flinging newspapers directly onto readers' doorsteps, haul newspapers to distribution centers and newsstands? Via a regulation, the Department of Labor has resolved this statutory ambiguity—concluding that those who haul newspapers for distribution *are* entitled to the statute's more far-reaching protections.[41]

In addition to resolving statutory ambiguities like this one, executive branch officials investigate violations of the statute and seek penalties against violators. All these activities help to put Congress's laws into effect. As such, they tend to fall clearly within modern understandings of the executive branch's power to execute the law.

Sometimes, however, members of the executive branch take actions that may look even less like *executing* the law (which is a job for the president) and more like *making* the law (which is a job for Congress). President Obama tested this line in his second term in office. In 2012, one of Obama's departments in the executive branch—the Department of Homeland Security (DHS)—announced that it would change its enforcement priorities and policies in response to concerns over "Dreamers," young people who had been brought illegally into the country as children.[42] Although statutes previously enacted by Congress gave DHS the power to deport these young people, the new DHS policy protected Dreamers from deportation if they could meet certain criteria. It also allowed them to apply for work authorization. DHS referred to this policy as Deferred Action for Childhood Arrivals, or DACA.

Even as Obama stressed the importance of these policy changes, he acknowledged that Congress had not enacted a statute implementing DACA or otherwise altering the nation's immigration laws. In this sense, he recognized that DACA was an end run around congressional inaction.[43] Such a bold use of executive power triggered fierce debate. According to its detractors, DHS's new policy constituted an impermissible attempt at making new law. Its supporters, by contrast, insisted that DHS was doing nothing more than exercising enforcement discretion in the course of executing the law.

As we will see in chapter 3—when we return to DACA while discussing the president's toolkit—these debates intensified in 2014 when DHS expanded the policy to reach even more undocumented immigrants. Ultimately, however, neither side achieved a definitive victory in the courts. As a result, some uncertainty continues to define the legal line that separates making the law from executing it.

From the perspective of the president, such blurriness around the margins of executive power is not necessarily a bad thing. Indeed, it is precisely the Constitution's lack of clarity that has helped presidents push and expand the bounds of executive power over time.[44] Nevertheless, as Truman learned from the *Youngstown* case, the reaches of executive power can only be stretched so far before the law pushes back.

The Power to Act as Commander in Chief

When a legal rule is blurry around the edges, lawyers often refer to that rule as being unsettled. This means that the rule raises legal questions that have no definitive or well-accepted answers. Any candid analysis of that legal rule must take such uncertainty into account. As we will discuss in chapter 6, such blurriness arises with particular frequency when the federal courts have not been able or willing to wade into particular controversies. In few areas of the law is this blurriness as pronounced as it is with respect to another power the Constitution grants to the president: that conferred by the Commander in Chief Clause.[45]

This clause, which designates the president the commander in chief of the armed forces, has inspired a wide range of interpretations. Some interpret the clause broadly, arguing that it provides legal support for "*any* Presidential action, internal or external, involving use of force, the idea being that it vests power to do anything, anywhere, that can be done with an army or navy."[46] This interpretation advances a truly sweeping conception of a president's powers. Others construe the clause far more narrowly, maintaining that it accomplishes nothing more than ensuring that the country's armed forces ultimately remain under the supervision of the president, rather than a military leader or some other authority.[47] This narrower interpretation assumes that a president will generally have to look elsewhere—to other constitutional provisions or to statutes—to support actions he might wish to take, even when those actions are related to the military. Many others argue that the proper understanding of the Commander in Chief Clause lies somewhere in the middle.

Perhaps unsurprisingly, most modern presidents have responded to these unresolved debates by arguing in favor of an expansive understanding of the Commander in Chief Clause. Still, even these presidents tend to hesitate before taking actions that might come close to the legal line. An example came in 2011, when President Obama decided to continue American military activities in Libya. Whether Obama had the legal authority to order these operations elicited controversy even from within his own administration, with top lawyers from two executive branch agencies (the Department of Defense and the Department of Justice) concluding that Obama did not have the authority. Other top lawyers, including those working within the State Department and the White House itself, reached the opposite conclusion. Obama ultimately sided with the latter group of government lawyers, maintaining that he did have legal authority to continue operations.[48] The process by which Obama reached this conclusion was telling. Even though Obama ultimately was willing to reject the conclusions of his own administration's lawyers in the course of deliberations, he felt it necessary to consult experts and to analyze the legal precedents. In other words, Obama still felt bound by the rule of law. Indeed, he felt bound even though he knew that—as we will discuss in chapter 6—the courts likely would never get involved.

Regardless of how these debates play out, legal experts tend to agree that at least one set of principles helps to define the contours of the president's commander in chief powers. Deriving from one justice's analysis in the *Youngstown* case, this set of principles holds that the president's authority is at its highest when Congress has enacted legislation purporting to authorize the president's use of the power in question. By contrast, the president's authority is at its lowest when Congress has enacted legislation disapproving of the president's use of that power. For actions between these two poles—actions taken by a president without congressional approval *or* disapproval—the president's authority is in a "zone of twilight," and it becomes particularly difficult to parse the precise legal limits.[49] Many have turned to this analytical framework to shed light not only on the scope of the authority the president enjoys by virtue of the Commander in Chief Clause, but also on the limits of the president's authority more generally.

In the context of the president as commander in chief, the balance struck by *Youngstown* reflects, among other things, the fact that the Constitution expressly grants some military-related powers not to the president but instead to Congress. The Constitution expressly gives Congress the power to declare war, for example, as well as the power to control military-related funding.[50] The Constitution, in other words, contemplates that the president and Congress will share responsibility for the country's military-related decisions.

The *Youngstown* framework helps to explain why the president has such sweeping legal authority to conduct military operations when Congress has given him express authority to do so. Three days after the

2001 terrorist attacks against the United States, for example, Congress passed a bill giving the president the power "to use all necessary and appropriate force against those nations, organizations, or persons he determines planned, authorized, committed, or aided the terrorist attacks that occurred on September 11, 2001."[51] Soon thereafter, President Bush relied on this statutory authority as the legal basis for ordering military operations in Afghanistan. Whether Bush's decision was correct as a matter of policy is not something that the law is able to answer. However, as a strictly legal matter, Congress's statute put Bush on very solid ground in concluding that he had the authority to order military action. Later, both Obama and Trump argued that this same statute—often referred to as the 2001 Authorization for Use of Military Force—provided legal authority for taking military action against ISIS. These more recent invocations of the 2001 statute have triggered far greater legal controversy and, as such, have increased the political pressure on Congress to enact an updated statute that more clearly defines the scope of Congress's authorization.

The *Youngstown* framework also helps to explain why Congress often turns to statutes when it is concerned with how presidents are running the military. In 1973, in the wake of controversy surrounding the Vietnam War, Congress passed the War Powers Resolution.[52] (It did so, tellingly, over the veto of President Nixon, who argued that the statute unconstitutionally interfered with his commander in chief powers.) The War Powers Resolution imposes various consulting and reporting requirements on the president to try to force him to engage with Congress when engaging in hostilities. It also restricts the president's ability to commit armed forces to military action for more than sixty days without obtaining congressional authorization. The War Powers Resolution, of course, did not bring an end to all power struggles between Congress and the president in matters of foreign affairs. However, it illustrates Congress's efforts to push back against the president's perceived encroachment on Congress's role.

Even more recently, some members of Congress have tried to clarify the law surrounding a more specific issue: the use of nuclear weapons. These legislators have focused on whether the commander in chief power allows a president to launch a nuclear attack even in the absence of congressional approval or an attack on the United States. Uncomfortable with this possibility, these lawmakers have proposed a statute that would make it clear that, absent a declaration of war by Congress, the president lacks the authority to launch a preemptive nuclear strike. The proposed legislation explains that nuclear weapons are uniquely powerful weapons and insists that the Constitution puts the "monumental decision to go to war" into the hands of the people's many representatives in Congress, not in the hands of a single president.[53] As of 2017, however, this legislation has not been enacted.

Another important constraint on the president's commander in chief power involves restrictions imposed by international law, including the Charter of the United Nations. Presidents often feel constrained by the restrictions that these international laws impose on their use of military force. Although there may be no legal consequences within U.S. law when a president violates these international rules, allegations of violations have in the past triggered international legal consequences. As a result, presidents seeking to authorize, or even threaten, military force often take pains to explain how their actions satisfy international law mandates.

Still, legal blurriness continues to define the meaning and scope of the Constitution's Commander in Chief Clause. For reasons we will discuss in chapter 6, the courts are unlikely to resolve these uncertainties anytime soon. As a result, difficult debates—regarding not only the wisdom of a president's military actions but also their legality—are left to unfold primarily before Congress, the president, and the public.

The Power to Negotiate Treaties

Another outward-facing power that the Constitution grants to the president is the ability to make treaties with foreign nations. The Constitution allows the president to exercise this power so long as two-thirds of senators cast their votes in support. Once ratified, a treaty has the force and effect of law, just like a law passed by Congress. The Senate has approved treaties involving a wide range of subjects: from migratory birds to the United Nations, from the Louisiana Purchase to nuclear weapons.

Throughout our country's history, the vast majority of treaties submitted by the president have received the Senate's approval. By one count, the Senate approved more than 1,500 treaties in its first 200 years—and rejected only twenty-one.[54] These statistics, however, are a bit misleading, as many potential treaties are never submitted to the Senate. This is because presidents—seeking to avoid the supermajority requirement in the Senate and all the political gridlock that comes along with it—have increasingly turned away from treaties and toward what are called executive agreements.

Executive agreements take two different forms. First, there are congressional-executive agreements, which require a simple majority vote in both houses of Congress, rather than a supermajority in the Senate. One prominent example of such an agreement is the North America Free Trade Agreement (NAFTA), an agreement between the United States, Canada, and Mexico that aims to facilitate trade between the three countries.

Second, there are sole executive agreements. The president enters into these agreements with foreign countries without seeking any congressional approval at all. One recent, high-profile example is the Paris Agreement—an agreement President Obama signed in 2016 in an effort to address global climate change. The White House called the Paris Agreement "the most ambitious climate change agreement in history."[55] However, Obama did not seek Congress's approval before entering it, and, in June 2017, President Trump stated his intention to remove the United States from the agreement.

Most legal experts agree that, in terms of U.S. law, a president has the power to unilaterally withdraw from a sole executive agreement, such as the Paris Agreement, without seeking congressional approval. This tracks an assumption among legal experts that the federal government has the power to amend or terminate international agreements in the same manner that they were made.

It may seem strange, as a legal matter, for a president to be able to avoid the Constitution's treaty requirements simply by turning to a different legal form—by signing an executive agreement, for example, rather than a treaty. Yet presidents have taken these liberties without triggering effective pushback by Congress, the courts, or other actors. As a practical matter, therefore, presidents have grown to enjoy extensive legal leeway in matters of foreign affairs.

Congress's Handoffs to the President: Delegation by Statute

Considered as a whole, the Constitution gives the president a great deal of authority. Yet as the *Youngstown* framework suggests, the Constitution is just the start. Congressional statutes also play a central role, as they grant the president tremendous and wide-ranging power. Indeed, every time Congress passes a statute, it affects (and generally expands) the president's ability to carry out his constitutionally appointed duty to execute the law.

Take, for example, the Clean Air Act of 1970. In passing and subsequently amending this law, Congress did not set permissible air-quality standards on its own. It did not slog through the expert-driven, tedious task of trying to figure out whether air-quality standards for carbon monoxide should be set at exactly 9 parts per million or 8 parts per million, or whether ozone should be set at 0.070 parts per million or 0.080 parts per million. Rather, Congress delegated that time-intensive, data-driven task to the administrator of the EPA—an individual who is nominated by, and can be fired by, the president. In empowering the administrator of the EPA to set national air-quality standards, Congress simply told the EPA in general terms to ensure that any primary standards would be "requisite to protect the public health" with "an adequate margin of safety."[56]

A statute like the Clean Air Act is deliberately vague because Congress wants the president or other actors within the executive branch to fill in the details left open in the statutory scheme. Congress, for example, might have found the issues too complex, too technical, or too politically difficult to answer on its own. Or Congress might have chosen to delegate broadly to allow regulators to respond to changing facts and circumstances in a flexible manner.

Regardless of the reason, the reality is that Congress routinely hands away vast amounts of power to executive branch agencies, and these delegations enable agencies to impose their conclusions about important policy matters onto the public. Agencies often accomplish this by issuing regulations. Many regulations have legally binding effects and, to that end, operate just like statutes do. In fact, it is possible to be sent to jail or fined for violating many agency regulations, even though agency regulations are not passed by Congress.[57]

How is this permissible? Legally speaking, agencies have the ability to issue regulations not because the Constitution allows them to make laws, but rather because Congress uses its own legislative power to create the agencies and empower them to issue regulations. As a result, when agencies enact regulations pursuant to Congress's directions (even very vague congressional directions), they are generally said to be *executing* the law made by Congress, not *making* the law.[58] For better or worse, the effect of this arrangement is to make it much easier for the federal government to develop comprehensive regulatory frameworks in response to our nation's challenges. Indeed, regulations are now such a central part of our governmental system that the number of regulations issued by federal agencies each year far eclipses the number of statutes enacted by Congress.

As an illustration, consider the problem of ensuring safe workplaces across our country—workplaces that involve everything from agriculture to manufacturing to construction. In 1970, Congress decided it was time to enact a statute to assure workers safe and healthy working conditions. To achieve this goal, Congress could have tried on its own to identify all sorts of different workplace hazards (involving ladders, chemicals, machinery, noise exposure, and any number of other disparate concerns), and it could have tried to set forth safety requirements to govern all of those many hazards, enacting new statutes whenever a new safety-related problem emerged. Yet that would have been difficult, time-consuming, and politically impractical. So instead of legislating with specificity, Congress passed a law—the Occupational Safety and Health Act of 1970—that in very general terms gave the secretary of labor the power to identify workplace hazards and to make binding workplace safety standards.[59] In other words, Congress assigned the job of actually identifying and regulating workplace hazards to the executive branch.

Although the Occupational Safety and Health Act was enacted nearly fifty years ago, it continues to empower the executive branch to this day. The Department of Labor still is able to make new, binding rules pursuant to Congress's delegation. In 2016, for example, the Occupational Safety and Health Administration (part of the Department of Labor) issued a rule aimed at limiting workers' exposure to silica dust so as to reduce lung cancer, silicosis, pulmonary disease, and kidney disease in America's workers.[60] These sorts of federal safety regulations all emanate from the Department of Labor—not from Congress.

There are, of course, limits on this power. Importantly, the executive branch can only exercise congressionally delegated powers in a manner that is consistent with the enabling statutes. The secretary of labor cannot, for example, use the Occupational Safety and Health Act to make a binding rule relating to banking regulations, clean energy, or immigration policy. Moreover, whenever agencies make binding rules, they generally must follow detailed procedural requirements set forth by Congress, as well as comply with any relevant constitutional provisions.

Despite these sorts of limits, delegations from Congress to the executive branch serve as an immensely important source of presidential power. They enable the executive branch to make binding rules—rules that protect all of us and that impose burdens on everyone. In addition, as we will discuss in chapter 3, the president has a limited but important ability to harness these enormous assignments of power to push forward his own agenda. Indeed, at least in the domestic arena, the powers granted to the executive branch by statutes—coupled with the president's constitutional duty to execute the laws—dwarf the president's other constitutional powers. In short, Congress has chosen, through statute, to hand the president a great deal of authority.

In Sum: The President's Powers Are Great, but Not Limitless

The president wields a tremendous amount of authority. Yet this power is not boundless. Rather, the president has power only because some source of law provides it. The Constitution serves as a major source of presidential power. It gives the president the ability to perform specific tasks like vetoing bills and nominating key government officials, and it also includes some fairly general and highly debated grants of authority, such as the provision empowering the president to act as the nation's commander in chief. In addition to these constitutional provisions, congressionally enacted statutes provide the executive branch with vast power, including the power to impose binding regulations on the public. Whether constitutional or statutory in origin, these grants of presidential power all come from some source of law. That same source of law also defines their limits.

Given that the law both empowers and constrains the president, determining whether a president's action is legal requires an answer to the following question: What *source of law*, if any, gives the president the power to take that action? If the president can locate a source of authority, then he may be able to achieve the change he desires. Yet this will happen only if the president can also provide an adequate answer to a second question: Namely, what *tool*, if any, can he use to take the action he wants to take? In our next chapter, we turn to this second inquiry.

CHAPTER 3

The President's Toolkit

Well, how exactly are you going to do that? ... What magic wand do you have?

— President Barack Obama, reacting to Donald Trump's 2016 campaign promises[1]

The American economy plodded along sluggishly as 2013 drew to a close. Political gridlock prevented Congress from getting much of anything done, and many Americans were struggling. By January 2014, President Obama had grown impatient. So the president gathered his high-ranking executive branch officials and announced that he planned to make progress, whether or not Congress acted.

"I've got a pen and I've got a phone," Obama declared. "And I can use that pen to sign executive orders and take executive actions and administrative actions that move the ball forward."[2]

Over the course of the following year, which Obama referred to as "a year of action,"[3] the president tested the limits of his executive powers. He signed an executive order that raised the minimum wage for federal contractors. He directed the Treasury Department to create a new retirement savings account for millions of Americans. He oversaw his administration's announcement of new carbon-pollution standards designed to address climate change. And he instructed the Department of Homeland Security, when enforcing the nation's immigration laws, to prioritize the deportation of those with serious criminal histories.[4] Notably, Obama attempted to do all this, and more, without Congress taking any additional steps to help him.

Instead, Obama tried to tackle this ambitious project with the powers already granted to him by statute or the Constitution, using the collection of tools found in the president's own toolkit. These presidential tools are varied. Some are informal and political in nature—such as coaxing, tweeting, and plain old arm-twisting. A president seeking to involve Congress might, for example, pressure legislators to enact new laws by promising to campaign for them at their next election.

Other presidential tools are much more formal and have some grounding in the law. Among the most important of these are the issuance of executive orders, presidential oversight over rulemaking, and enforcement discretion. A president can use these tools individually or in combination. All three play an important role in helping the president carry out his constitutional powers, especially his overarching power to execute the laws. Still, any attempt to use these tools—and certainly any attempt to achieve "a year of action" without the support of Congress—is likely to be marked by both successes and failures. This is because legal limits constrain a president's ability to employ his tools, just as they constrain all presidential actions.

By the Stroke of a Pen: Executive Orders

Executive orders serve as a major tool in a president's toolkit. The principal purpose of these written instruments is straightforward: To successfully follow through on his constitutional duty to "take Care that the Laws be faithfully executed,"[5] the president needs an effective means of communicating with those working beneath him within the executive branch. Executive orders fill this need by giving the president a formal way of telling executive branch officials what they should, or should not, do while they work to administer and enforce the nation's laws.[6] In response to these sorts of orders, these high-ranking officials tend to sit up and listen. Many of them, after all, were handpicked by the president and work at his pleasure.

To create an executive order, a president generally needs to simply write something up, sign it at the bottom, and publish it in the *Federal Register*. (The *Federal Register*, which can be found online at www.federalregister.gov, serves as the official daily journal for the U.S. government.) The same process applies if a president wishes to change or withdraw an old executive order, including one issued by a predecessor.

What this means is that executive orders do not go through the legislative process that laws passed by Congress go through. Nor do they require congressional approval. In this sense, a president really can create—or wipe away—an executive order with the mere "stroke of a pen."[7]

This might seem startling until one realizes that most executive orders are not legally binding. That is, most executive orders do not legally compel anyone to act, and they are not enforceable in court. Instead, most executive orders are "enforceable" only to the extent that the president chooses to exert political pressure on those charged with carrying them out.

Nonetheless, presidents do sometimes issue executive orders that have legally binding effects on government actors, as well as on private citizens. Whether a president can issue this kind of order depends on the legal limits we discussed in chapters 1 and 2. Specifically, when a president issues an executive order that purports to have legally binding effect, he must be able to demonstrate that the order complies with all legal restrictions (including, for example, that it complies with the First Amendment, the Due Process Clause, and other constitutional mandates). In addition, the president must be able to demonstrate that it has been authorized by some underlying, preexisting legal authority.[8] To demonstrate the latter, the president normally has to point to something in either the Constitution or a congressional statute.[9] Without this authorization, an executive order likely will have no legal effect at all.

Viewed as a whole, the Constitution and statutes currently on the books tend to give the president the most power to act in matters involving government employees, federal contracts, military policy, and overall executive branch administration. As a result, these areas tend to be subject to a great deal of regulation through presidents' executive orders and other unilateral directives. The very first executive order provides an illustration. Issued by President Washington in 1789, this order involved executive branch administration. More specifically, it requested that high-ranking executive branch officials provide the president, in writing, with an accounting of their departments' recent work.[10] This order easily fell within the president's constitutionally granted powers, given that the Constitution makes him the head of the executive branch and also expressly gives him the power to request opinions in writing from the heads of executive branch departments.[11] As such, the order was legally authorized.

Many modern executive orders are similarly structured. While their commands might reach more broadly than Washington's 1789 order, they still target matters of internal government and, as a result, tend to fall squarely within the president's constitutional or statutory powers. For example, in 1948, President Truman relied in part on his constitutional power as commander in chief to issue an order that desegregated the military.[12] In 1969, President Nixon cited both constitutional and statutory authority in support of an executive order that protected federal government workers from employment discrimination based on "race, color, religion, sex, or national origin."[13] Subsequent presidents have expanded on Nixon's order to protect against other forms of discrimination, and collectively these orders still to this day provide protection in federal employment.[14] Even more recently, during his so-called "year of action," Obama cited both his constitutional and statutory powers in support of an executive order that raised the minimum wage to $10.10 per hour for federal contractors—meaning those who enter into contracts with the federal government to provide labor, materials, and other services.[15]

All these orders were aimed at government affairs, such as government contracts and government employment. Other executive orders, by contrast, are not so narrowly confined. Instead, they purport to extend beyond the government's own affairs and directly regulate private individuals and private conduct.[16] These orders tend to be more controversial—and more legally problematic. Trump's January 2017 travel ban order provides a striking example of such a far-reaching order, as it directly affected nongovernmental actors all over the world. Whether the law allows a president's order to reach this far depends on whether some preexisting statute or constitutional grant of authority empowers the president to act as he did. It further depends on whether the president's order complies with various constitutional commands, such as the First Amendment's insistence that the government not establish a religion. If the order passes both of these tests, then normally its issuance is legal, and its commands can bind even private individuals. If not, then normally its issuance is illegal, and a court will refuse to approve its enforcement.

The Supreme Court has recognized these legal limitations, and it has ruled accordingly. In 1936, for example, the court considered whether President Franklin D. Roosevelt had the power to issue an order that, in effect, turned previously legal activity into a criminal offense.[17] More specifically, Roosevelt's 1936 order announced a prohibition on selling arms to Bolivia or Paraguay. Violating this prohibition could land the perpetrator in jail. After Roosevelt issued the order, federal prosecutors accused a private company of violating its terms by selling machine guns to Bolivia. In response, the company argued that the president lacked the power to issue the order in the first place.

The court sided with Roosevelt. However, it did not do so under the theory that the president may do whatever he wants simply by issuing a unilateral order. To the contrary, the court reasoned that the president's 1936 order was legal and enforceable because it was expressly authorized by Congress, and it involved a matter of foreign affairs, where the president's powers are at their peak. This case, *United States v. Curtiss-Wright Export Corporation,*[18] frequently is cited as an example of just how far a president's authority extends. Yet even it confirmed the fundamental limits on what a president can do. It confirmed that a president can act only if some source of legal authority allows him to take that action.

A half century later, this same principle thwarted an effort at reform by President Bill Clinton. In 1995, Clinton signed an executive order meant to protect workers. This order prohibited the federal government from contracting with certain companies that replaced striking employees. As noted above, constitutional and statutory law tends to give the president a great deal of power in the area of federal contracts, and this helped to support Clinton's conclusion that he had the legal authority to issue this executive order. Clinton's critics, however, reached the opposite conclusion. They argued that a congressional statute—the National Labor Relations Act— limited the president's power in this particular context. More specifically, they argued that the statute limited the president's power to interfere with an employer's right to hire permanent replacements during labor strikes.

A federal appellate court eventually agreed with Clinton's critics. It reached this result after concluding that no source of law had authorized Clinton's 1995 order—and that the National Labor Relations Act actually prohibited it. As a result, Clinton did not have the legal authority to issue the order, and it could not be enforced.[19]

Clinton's experience—coupled with the experiences of presidents before and after him—confirms that the law does, indeed, constrain a president's ability to act, even through executive orders. Yet sometimes a president's goal in issuing an executive order is not to achieve legal gains but rather to advance political ends. In other words, sometimes a president issues executive orders to make the headlines or to curry favor with voters, even if he knows the orders do not have much legal effect. Consider, for example, the executive order Trump signed on his very first day in office. The news media described this order, which aimed to minimize the burdens of the Affordable Care Act (a.k.a. Obamacare) in dramatic terms. "Trump takes the ax to Obamacare with his first Oval Office order," the *Daily Mail* announced. "He signs directive making explicit he WILL repeal and replace."[20] The *New York Times* followed suit: "Trump Issues Executive Order Scaling Back Parts of Obamacare."[21]

Yet Trump's January 20 order did not itself scale back any part of the Affordable Care Act, much less repeal or replace it. Instead, the order merely directed the heads of executive agencies to take whatever actions they could, "*consistent with law*," to "minimize the unwarranted economic and regulatory burdens of the Act."[22] It instructed agency heads, no fewer than three times, to take some action and then, in the same breath, qualified those instructions by telling the agencies to act to the "maximum extent permitted by law."[23] The applicable "law" here included the Affordable Care Act itself, as well as various statutes that speak to the cumbersome and time-consuming procedures that agencies must use when issuing regulations. As a result, Trump's first executive order made a big political splash, but it had basically no legal effect.

In sum, executive orders give presidents a way to communicate, in an official way, with members of the executive branch. Presidents frequently use this tool to provide directions to those working beneath them and to govern matters of internal government affairs. Sometimes presidents will issue executive orders that go beyond internal government and affect private actors in very serious ways. Regardless of how far an order reaches, however, each executive order needs some support in, and must be consistent with, the law. The power to issue executive orders is merely a tool. It is not a license to rule by decree.

All the President's Fingerprints:
Presidential Oversight over Rulemaking

As we have discussed, the law gives the president the ability to issue legally binding executive orders—but only up to a point. A president must ground these directives in some source of legal authority. As it turns out, Congress only occasionally gives power to the president himself to issue orders that directly regulate private individuals.[24]

Things are very different, however, for administrative agencies. These agencies, such as the Department of Energy and the Department of Labor, are part of the executive branch, and they are created and empowered by Congress. Whereas Congress only occasionally gives unilateral regulatory power to the president in name, Congress frequently chooses to give agencies like these sweeping legal authority to create rules that regulate private individuals.

Imagine how enticing this must be to a president: An agency, which the president supervises, has expressly been given the power to regulate people and entities all across the country. So much power—and yet it is just out of reach! This arrangement helps to explain why presidents have, over time, become increasingly forceful in their attempts to control the rulemaking activities of federal agencies. This phenomenon is often referred to as regulatory oversight, and its history demonstrates how it works.

In the early 1980s, President Reagan laid the foundation for modern-day regulatory oversight by demanding that the White House play a role in overseeing agencies' regulatory activities. He accomplished this by issuing an executive order setting forth his instructions. Reagan justified the legal authority for White House review in very general terms, referring to the authority vested in him "as President by the Constitution and laws of the United States of America."[25] The order stirred controversy among legal scholars and others, who debated whether the president had the legal authority to call for this review. Notwithstanding this debate, later presidents, most notably Presidents Clinton and Obama, expanded on Reagan's efforts, and, as a result, White House review became entrenched. It is now commonplace for presidents to require executive agencies to submit major rules to the White House for review and approval before a proposed or final rule can be issued. (Note that the same review requirements do *not* apply to independent agencies whose leadership enjoys some insulation from presidential control due to congressionally conferred job protections.)

In addition, modern presidents often will go so far as to suggest—to the press, to their constituents, and even to those in the government— that an agency's regulatory decision is somehow the president's own to make. President Obama, for example, suggested that a decision about regulating power plants was his to make, even though the relevant statute required that the decision be made not by the president but rather by the Environmental Protection Agency. Obama did so both by exerting pressure on the EPA to reach the result he wanted and by suggesting to the public that he was personally responsible for the outcome.[26] Such heavy-handed presidential involvement can confuse observers, who may not understand who has the ultimate authority for the decision. Despite the political rhetoric, the legal answer is clear: If the statute gave the legal authority to the agency, then it remains with the agency. Admittedly, the heads of these agencies often work at the president's pleasure. Still, there remains an important legal distinction between the president and his agency heads.

The trend toward more aggressive forms of regulatory oversight by presidents has sparked extensive legal debate.[27] Recall that any presidential action must have some grounding in the law. So what law, constitutional or statutory, allows a president to exert such pressure on administrative agencies? Those defending a more aggressive presidential approach often cite various constitutional powers, including the Take Care Clause. As we discussed in chapter 2, this Clause requires the president to "take Care that the Laws be faithfully executed."[28] Those defending a more aggressive approach also tend to cite the president's power to remove executive branch officials. By contrast, those who challenge strong presidential control tend to point to Congress's decision to place power with an expert agency, not with the president himself. Notwithstanding these ongoing debates among legal experts, each president has further entrenched aggressive regulatory oversight. It is now baked into the regulatory structure.[29]

Once again, however, regulatory oversight has its legal limits. A president cannot simply direct administrative agencies to do whatever he wants. This is because Congress is the authority that, directly or indirectly, creates and empowers all federal agencies. Indeed, "the entire machinery of the executive arm of the United States government below the level of the President is the result of congressional action."[30] When Congress takes legislative action to create and empower agencies, Congress generally does not require that agencies follow the *president's* instructions. Instead, Congress generally requires that agencies carefully follow *Congress's* statutory instructions. If agencies fail to follow Congress's instructions, their actions may be struck down if challenged in court.

As an example, a congressionally enacted statute called the Administrative Procedure Act often directs agencies to employ a highly technical process before they can make a new regulation or repeal an old one.[31] This process is called notice-and-comment rulemaking. If agencies fail to follow these congressional requirements, their regulations may be invalidated if challenged in court. Notice-and-comment rulemaking begins when an agency publishes a notice of a proposed rule in the *Federal Register*. That notice must disclose key information that the agency relied on in developing the proposed rule,[32] and it must explain how and where members of the public can file comments in response. Publication of this notice begins what is called the comment period. During this period, members of the public—including you, and anyone else interested—can share their thoughts about the proposed rule with the agency. (Often the process of filing a comment is as simple as visiting www.regulations.gov, the federal government's online rulemaking portal.) Congress then requires that the agency consider and respond to all significant comments when finalizing the rule.[33] Once the comment period closes and the agency completes its review, it publishes the text of its final rule in the *Federal Register*, along with a statement that thoroughly explains the agency's reasoning and responds to the public's comments.[34]

Fulfilling these procedural requirements takes a great deal of time, effort, and coordination. In fact, it is not unusual for a major rulemaking proceeding to stretch on for months or sometimes even years. If at any point in this process the agency makes a mistake, that error might very well trigger legal challenges and require the agency to start all over.

Jumping through these procedural hoops can be difficult. Yet even successful navigation of these procedural obstacles is not enough to turn a proposed rule into an enforceable regulation. This is because an agency is legally allowed to impose a new rule only if Congress granted it power to do so. The same applies if an agency wishes to change or eliminate an existing rule. This means that the agency must demonstrate that its change in the rules is consistent with the text of the congressionally enacted laws that the agency purports to be putting into effect. These statutes often require, among other things, that the agency identify studies, legal language, data, or other expert-driven considerations in support of its newly developed rule, as well as in support of its decision to repeal or amend existing rules. A court might well strike down a rule, labeling it "arbitrary and capricious," if an agency fails to consider relevant factors, or if it considers factors that the statute does not allow it to consider.[35] For example, if an agency were bold enough to justify a rule (or the elimination of a rule) by simply saying "our boss, the president, told us to," it would almost certainly prompt a successful legal challenge.[36] Alternatively, if an agency—either on its own initiative or due to presidential prodding—were to try to regulate in an area that Congress had not given it the power to touch, a court could strike down the rule as in excess of the agency's statutorily granted authority.

For purposes of illustration, consider a dispute involving the following three players: the tobacco industry, the Food and Drug Administration (FDA), and President Bill Clinton. As Clinton was preparing for his 1996 reelection campaign, he wanted to win political points by regulating tobacco and curtailing underage smoking. Clinton knew he did not have the legal authority to impose this regulation himself. Neither the Constitution nor a statute gave him that authority. Instead, Clinton's best legal shot at achieving this reform was to convince the FDA, an executive branch agency, to use its own statutory authority granted by Congress to regulate in the way he desired. As such, Clinton publicly directed the FDA to develop his preferred regulations.[37] Throughout the regulatory process, Clinton kept up the pressure and continued claiming the work as his own. When the FDA was still working to finalize its rule on the subject, for example, Clinton's reelection campaign emphasized Clinton's efforts to protect children from smoking and attacked his opponent's stance on tobacco.

On the heels of these campaign statements, the FDA declared that it had the statutory authority to regulate tobacco and that it had finalized a rule on the subject. Then, when the FDA issued its final rule, Clinton personally took credit. "Today, we are taking direct action to protect our children from tobacco and especially the advertising that hooks children on a product," Clinton announced while standing next to children wearing red "Tobacco-Free Kids" T-shirts at a Rose Garden ceremony.[38] Observers would be forgiven for concluding that Clinton had imposed this regulation himself. Yet, to be clear, Clinton did no such thing. Under the law, all he could do was encourage the FDA to impose the rule using powers Congress had already granted to the agency—and then, for the purpose of scoring political points, try to take personal credit for it.

Not surprisingly, the tobacco companies were not thrilled with this development. They filed suit in federal court, arguing that the rule exceeded the power Congress had granted to the FDA. The U.S. Supreme Court, splitting 5–4, agreed with the tobacco industry. At the outset of its opinion, the court's five-justice majority acknowledged that the case involved "one of the most troubling public health problems facing our Nation today: the thousands of premature deaths that occur each year because of tobacco use."[39] Yet after reviewing various laws passed by Congress, the majority concluded that Congress had "clearly precluded the FDA from asserting jurisdiction to regulate tobacco products," and so they struck down the rule.[40] In other words, the court concluded that Congress's statutes did not give the FDA the authority to enact the regulation. As a result, Clinton's efforts to regulate tobacco ultimately came to naught.

Years later, in 2009, a different president—Barack Obama—finally made progress on the problem of underage smoking. Yet Obama's success was not due to increased pressure on the FDA, more creative litigation tactics, or more forceful unilateral action. Rather, it was because Congress had finally stepped in. Earlier that same year, Congress had passed the Family Smoking Prevention and Tobacco Control Act.[41] This law gave the FDA the power it did not have in the 1990s—the power to regulate tobacco products.

This kind of push and pull between presidents and agencies—which is driven so fundamentally by the statutes passed by Congress—has become inescapable in modern American politics. Presidents continue to try to influence how agencies regulate, and those opposed to an agency's actions continue to try to push back through political pressure, regulatory participation, and court challenges. Almost immediately on taking office, President Trump perpetuated this pattern by actively overseeing and directing agency regulation. Unlike Clinton and Obama, however, Trump actively pursued a *deregulatory* agenda. This approach was consistent with his rhetoric before the election, during which he derided regulations as "job killers."[42]

In his first 100 days, Trump tried to fulfill his deregulatory promises by issuing a flurry of agency-directed instructions. He directed the Department of Labor to rethink a controversial Obama-era rule regulating retirement advisers.[43] He set forth core principles to guide the regulation of the financial system.[44] He directed the EPA to reconsider an Obama-era rule that regulates U.S. waters.[45] He ordered the review of fuel economy standards.[46] In addition, in one of his most controversial moves, he directed that all executive agencies remove two existing regulations from the books any time they decide to make a new regulation.[47] This order, which is referred to as Trump's "one-in, two-out" order, immediately prompted a court challenge.

It is hard to know what, if anything, will eventually come of all these directives. Trump presumably issued them with the hope that the agencies will follow them to the letter. Yet, as noted, the rulemaking process is complex, and achieving reform through the regulatory machinery is time-consuming and legally difficult. As Clinton's attempts to regulate tobacco suggest, sometimes a president's desired reform goes beyond what is legally authorized. Even if such a reform makes it through the agency, it may end up defeated in the courts.

The Power of Prioritization: Enforcement Decisions

A third significant tool in the president's toolkit involves what is known as enforcement discretion. The Constitution, as we have discussed, charges the president with taking care that the nation's laws are faithfully executed. The trouble is that we have so many federal statutes and regulations that the federal government cannot possibly enforce them all, against all violators, at all times. It would be logistically impossible. As a result, the Constitution's Take Care Clause has been read to give the executive branch significant discretion in deciding which enforcement actions should be prioritized and which should not. This is what "enforcement discretion" refers to: the discretion that the president and his officers have to decide when, and whether, to prosecute certain cases against individual violators.

To put this in perspective, consider the task facing the Internal Revenue Service (IRS), which is an agency, run by a presidential appointee, that consists of approximately 80,000 employees. Collectively, these employees need to interpret and apply more than ten million words of highly technical language found in the federal tax code and its accompanying regulations.[48] They also need to enforce all those tax laws and regulations against many millions of taxpayers. Each attempt at enforcement requires a great deal of time and effort, and IRS agents must adhere to strict protocols and procedures when bringing enforcement actions.[49] By no stretch of the imagination can these employees be expected to uncover every single violation of this vast set of rules. Instead, they must decide which investigations and enforcement proceedings to prioritize.

The IRS is far from alone in facing such a predicament. Limited resources necessarily force those working throughout the executive branch to prioritize certain actions over others. Given the president's supervisory role over executive branch activity, this gives him the opportunity not only to tweak enforcement priorities, but to do so in a way that advances his own political ends.

A president might turn to enforcement discretion, for example, to advance his preferred immigration policies. For example, he might direct the Department of Homeland Security to try to enforce the federal immigration laws against *all* undocumented people who have committed crimes, and not just against those who have committed more serious offenses. Such an instruction would be similar to the one President Trump gave when he first entered the White House.[50] Normally, when a president takes steps like this, he is acting squarely within the law.

The same is true of lower-ranking officials making routine enforcement decisions. For example, perhaps a federal prosecutor working within the Department of Justice decides not to prosecute a low-level drug offender. This might be because the prosecutor has concluded that the evidence was not strong enough, or perhaps she thought it appropriate to focus her energies on prosecuting the offender's suppliers or violent coconspirators. In reaching an individualized decision like this, the official is simply deciding on a case-by-case basis whether a particular prosecution warrants the government's limited time and resources. Federal officials cannot avoid making prioritizations of this sort, and normally these sorts of decisions are perfectly legal.

Still, sometimes when a president or his officials try to use enforcement discretion to achieve broad political ends, their actions come close to, or even cross, legal lines. Imagine a high-ranking official announcing that she will prohibit anyone in her department from enforcing any statute that does not further the president's policy goals. Perhaps the politically disfavored statutes protect the environment, in the case of the Environmental Protection Agency, or penalize those who violate civil rights, in the case of the Department of Justice. On the one hand, these statutes (enacted by the legislative branch) remain on the books; no one in the government has removed or altered them. On the other hand, these statutes (enforced, if at all, by the executive branch) have become a practical dead letter. There is a real tension between what the statutes require and how the executive branch is treating those requirements. Broad nonenforcement decisions of this sort raise thorny legal questions, including whether the executive branch really is still just *executing* the law—or whether, by declining to enforce rules and regulations in large categories of cases, it is now changing, repealing, or otherwise *making* the law.

Often, the courts stay out of debates over nonenforcement decisions, leaving it up to Congress and the president to work out any disagreements.[51] However, the courts occasionally will wade in. One consequential example involves the federal courts' review of Obama-era efforts to protect certain undocumented immigrants from deportation. As we discussed briefly in chapter 2, President Obama's administration implemented a policy called DACA in 2012 to aid certain undocumented childhood arrivals. It developed this policy in response to congressional inaction.

This was not the Obama Administration's only effort at immigration reform. Throughout his presidency, Obama repeatedly encouraged Congress to be the one to fix what he called a "broken" immigration system. By 2013, these calls had become more forceful. "Our economy is stronger when we harness the talents and ingenuity of striving, hopeful immigrants," Obama declared at his State of the Union address. "And right now, leaders from the business, labor, law enforcement, and faith communities all agree that the time has come to pass comprehensive immigration reform. Now is the time to do it. Now is the time to get it done."[52]

Try as he might, Obama was unable to prod Congress to pass laws that would implement comprehensive immigration reform. So on November 20, 2014, Obama went before the cameras and explained to the entire nation that, even though he continued to believe that a legislative fix was in order, he was tired of waiting for Congress to act. He was again going to take matters into his own hands.

Most dramatically, Obama directed government officials at DHS to broaden DACA and develop enforcement priorities that would avoid the deportation not only of undocumented children but also of millions of undocumented parents. Obama claimed that this shift in enforcement priorities would constitute nothing more than a lawful exercise of the executive branch's discretion in enforcement. In Obama's view, he was simply directing the government officials who enforce the federal immigration laws to focus their time and efforts away from these individuals and toward others who posed more of a threat to the nation's security. Focus on "felons, not families," Obama insisted. "Criminals, not children; gang members, not a mom who's working hard to provide for her kids."[53]

In response, DHS issued a memo outlining a policy of deferred action for millions of undocumented parents. It called this policy Deferred Action for Parents of Americans and Lawful Permanent Residents, or DAPA. While DHS's memo claimed that the agency would exercise its enforcement discretion on a case-by-case basis, some understood the policy as operating more broadly: as ensuring that DHS would not enforce the immigration laws against *any* parent who met DAPA's criteria.

Critics pounced. They argued that DAPA amounted to a rewriting of the immigration laws, something only Congress could do. "He tried to go around Congress with an executive order to rewrite laws unilaterally," Representative Paul Ryan complained. "Presidents don't write laws. Congress writes laws."[54]

In response, Texas and twenty-five other states filed suit, insisting that DHS had crossed a legal line. At preliminary stages of the case, *Texas v. United States*,[55] the state challengers won, and the federal courts forced the Obama Administration to put the DAPA policy on hold. The district court judge who first ruled in the case concluded that DHS's enforcement policy set forth a new substantive rule rather than simply a shift in enforcement priorities. As a new substantive rule, it needed to go through the Administrative Procedure Act's lengthy notice-and-comment requirements. Over the dissent of one judge, an appellate court agreed with the district court judge. It further reasoned that DHS's enforcement policy likely ran contrary to the instructions Congress had set forth in a statute called the Immigration and Nationality Act.

When the *Texas* case went up to the Supreme Court, a 4–4 tie among the justices (shorthanded by Justice Scalia's death in February 2016) prevented the court from providing clarification. As a result, the lower courts' opinions remained in effect, and the Obama Administration was not able to implement DAPA or otherwise use enforcement discretion as a tool to shield large categories of undocumented parents from deportation proceedings.

In June 2017, the Trump Administration announced that, regardless of the court proceedings, it was rescinding the DAPA policy altogether. DHS then took things a step further in September 2017 by rescinding the original 2012 nonenforcement policy—that is, by rescinding DACA, which had sought to shield undocumented children. Although the *Texas* lawsuit had not challenged the 2012 policy, the Trump Administration explained its decision to rescind DACA by pointing to the *Texas* case and noting that DACA and DAPA shared legal similarities. Opponents of the Trump Administration's rescission of DACA filed suit almost immediately. They argued, among other things, that DHS's changed views on DACA violated similar procedural requirements that, ironically, had tripped up DAPA.

The legal arguments surrounding DAPA and DACA are highly technical and remain unsettled. On a more general level, however, they confirm that enforcement discretion constitutes a potent tool in the president's toolkit—but that it, like all the others, has legal limits. If a president uses nonenforcement decisions too aggressively, legal questions are likely to arise. In response to these debates, lawyers and others must closely analyze what the executive branch is doing in order to determine, among other things, if the relevant statutes allow the executive branch to make the decisions at issue. This is because the president cannot make new law, even through enforcement decisions. Only the power to execute the law belongs to the president and those working beneath him.

In Sum: The President Has Many Tools but No Magic Wand

When a president seeks to execute the law, he has many tools to exercise his power. These include the issuance of executive orders, pressure over agency rulemaking, and discretion in enforcement.

Still, these tools do not change the general rule, which is that a president can only rarely advance an agenda all on his own. Nor do they affect the overarching principle of presidential power, which is that a president is not above the law but instead may take legally binding action only when some preexisting legal authority allows him to do so. That authority normally must derive from a statute or the Constitution. If that authority does not exist, even a president's most potent tools will have no legal effect.

One theme running throughout these discussions is the importance that legislation has on the powers of the president. By enacting or amending statutes—and by exercising its other powers—Congress can drastically alter a president's role in government. Our next chapter, accordingly, moves from the White House to the Capitol Building, where hundreds of members of Congress and their staff members are at work, continuously affecting how our government operates.

CHAPTER 4

How Congress Checks the President

We're going to do everything—and I mean everything we can do— to kill it, stop it, slow it down, whatever we can.

— Representative John Boehner explaining in 2010 how congressional Republicans planned to respond to President Obama's policy agenda[1]

George H.W. Bush had won the prime speaking slot at the 1988 Republican National Convention. As the candidate poised to become the party's official nominee for president, Bush knew the stakes were high. For years, he had been serving as a relatively quiet and uninspiring vice president to Ronald Reagan. In response, *Time* magazine suggested Bush might be a "pandering man with no mind of his own,"[2] while *Newsweek* chronicled his image as a wimp.[3] Bush needed this convention speech to improve his image. So the candidate was ready with a zinger.

"My opponent won't rule out raising taxes," Bush declared, halfway through his speech. "But I will. And the Congress will push me to raise taxes, and I'll say no. And they'll push, and I'll say no. And they'll push again, and I'll say to them"—Bush paused for effect—"read my lips. *No. New. Taxes.*"[4]

The crowd erupted; the line was a hit. The speech gave the Republican candidate a bounce in the polls. And it all paid off in November when Bush won the presidency.

Soon thereafter, Bush's prediction came to pass: Congress began pressuring him to approve tax increases. Yet in response, Bush went off script. Just over two years after he had so memorably asked voters to read his lips, Bush acquiesced to Congress's pressure and signed a bill that imposed—much to the dismay of his supporters—new taxes.

The relationship between Congress and the president is intense, messy, and complicated. Still, one thing is clear. Even the most forceful chief executives, and even the most emphatic presidential promises, can crumble when set against the powers wielded by the 535 voting members of Congress.

Much of what a president seeks to accomplish needs the support of Congress. The president needs this support not just in an informal sense but as a matter of law. If a president wants to see a new law put on the books (or an old one taken off), he needs Congress to enact a statute. If the president wants to keep the federal government running, he needs Congress to allocate money. If the president wants to fill a seat on the Supreme Court, he needs to obtain the Senate's approval. The list goes on. As a result, Congress poses a significant and continuing obstacle to any president's agenda.

Five points of congressional leverage are among the most important: those associated with legislation, spending, confirmations, oversight, and impeachment. Each of these levers gives Congress significant power over the president. This power wielded by Congress, in turn, gives each individual in the country more power over the president. This is because members of Congress are, by constitutional design, held accountable in elections that give voters additional opportunities to influence their government.

The Legislative Gatekeeper: Congress's Power to Make Law

The Constitution expressly places the power to make law in the hands of Congress, not the president.[5] As a result, many—perhaps most—presidential campaign promises can be achieved only with Congress's cooperation.

In the 2016 presidential campaign, for example, Democratic candidate Hillary Clinton pledged to eliminate tuition for certain college students. Libertarian candidate Gary Johnson supported the legalization of marijuana across the country. Green Party candidate Jill Stein vowed to move to a single-payer public health insurance program. If elected, perhaps each of these candidates would have worked hard to convince Congress to support these measures. However, as a matter of law, every one of these campaign proposals would have required Congress, not the president, to enact statutes to implement the promised changes.

The laws that Congress does enact have a tremendous impact on the powers wielded by the president and others in the executive branch. Sometimes laws passed by Congress constrain the president. A recent illustration came in the summer of 2017, when Congress passed a bill that imposed sanctions on Iran, North Korea, and Russia and restricted the president's ability to lift some of those sanctions. The bill passed both houses of Congress with bipartisan, veto-proof majorities. President Trump, calling the bill "seriously flawed," argued that it "encroache[d] on the executive branch's authority to negotiate."[6] The president nevertheless signed the bill into law, presumably because he knew Congress had the votes to override a veto.

Other laws enacted by Congress expand a president's power. For example, when Congress enacted the Affordable Care Act in 2010, it not only imposed significant changes on the health-care industry; it also transferred a sweeping collection of new powers and responsibilities to the executive branch. As a practical matter, the Affordable Care Act needed to transfer this authority—for how else could the federal government possibly implement and enforce such a vast new regulatory program? These new powers and responsibilities extended to various executive branch departments, including the Department of Health and Human Services and the Department of the Treasury. Given that the heads of those agencies report directly to the president, the Affordable Care Act did what so many other statutes do: It significantly expanded the power of the presidency.

While these examples illustrate that Congress can exert enormous power over the president through legislation, there is a catch. Enacting legislation is not easy. To the contrary, it is extraordinarily difficult.

To understand why, consider the legislative process. For Congress to pass a law, hundreds of people need to agree on what to regulate and how, right down to the last nitty-gritty textual detail. More specifically, the Constitution requires that hundreds of members of Congress (a majority of the Senate, joined with a majority of the House of Representatives) come together and all agree to vote in favor of the passage of the exact same legislative language. At that point, either the president signs the proposed legislation and it becomes a law, or the president vetoes it and, in most cases, it goes back to Congress. Congress then needs to wrangle up the votes of a supermajority of representatives, and a supermajority of senators, in order to override the president's veto and turn the bill into law.[7]

Shepherding a bill through this process is a monumental task. Imagine gathering hundreds of people you know and getting them all to agree to something that is both important and politically contentious. Now imagine doing it with the same number of politicians, each being pulled in a different direction, from all across the country.

And yet there is more. A byzantine collection of procedural rules further complicates the legislative process. These rules do not come from the Constitution but rather are of Congress's own making. Frequently, these procedural rules make it even harder to vote on proposed laws and, as a result, even harder to enact legislation. As a result of these hurdles, members of Congress often do not get the opportunity even to vote on legislation they might favor.

An important example of these procedural rules relates to what is often referred to as a filibuster. A filibuster is a way for senators to block a proposed statute from going to a vote. The most famous form of the filibuster is the talking filibuster. As the name suggests, it involves talking. A lot of it. Basically, a senator (or group of senators working together in a tag-team fashion) takes the Senate floor and engages in prolonged debate to try to block a vote from ever taking place. A talking filibuster generally ends only when the speakers eventually grow tired and give up, or when three-fifths of the Senate vote to end the debate. Given this three-fifths requirement, a minority of senators can potentially block proposed legislation from ever coming to a vote.

Senator Strom Thurmond, a segregationist from South Carolina, holds the current record for the longest individual filibuster speech. In 1957, he held the Senate floor for twenty-four hours and eighteen minutes in an attempt to stall passage of the Civil Rights Act of 1957.[8] The act eventually passed despite his efforts to block it.

Much more recently, in 2013, Senator Ted Cruz commandeered the Senate floor for more than twenty-one hours. He did so not to block any vote in particular (as is the case with most traditional filibusters) but rather to engage in what was derided as a "faux" filibuster to protest the Affordable Care Act. To pass the time during his twenty-one-hour marathon, Cruz "discussed Ashton Kutcher and Toby Keith, did a Darth Vader impression, recited passages from Ayn Rand," and read Dr. Seuss's *Green Eggs and Ham* as a bedtime story for his daughters in case they were watching via C-SPAN.[9]

Today, Senate rules allow senators to call for a filibuster without even having to stay present on the Senate floor. This tweak in the rules has dramatically increased the ease with which filibusters can be deployed. As a result, a minority of senators often have the ability to prevent a majority from pushing through bills that lack bipartisan support.

Senate rules do not allow for the possibility of a filibuster for all legislation. This helps to explain why President Trump was able, in the first few months of his presidency, to sign into law over a dozen repeals of Obama-era regulations. Given the particular timing of their passage, each of these repeals was able to proceed to a vote based on special rules (set by a statute called the Congressional Review Act) that give Congress the ability to circumvent procedural hurdles like the filibuster.

Technically, it is possible for a bare Senate majority to eliminate the threat of the filibuster for all legislation going forward. As of 2017, however, Senate norms and other considerations have dissuaded the Senate from taking such a step.

The filibuster helps to illustrate both the power of Congress and its limits. On the one hand, the president needs Congress to get done what he wants, given that Congress is the branch with the power to enact legislation. On the other hand, Congress faces significant challenges whenever it attempts to pass a new law. As a result of this tension, if a statute does not already exist when a president takes office, then the president may very well have to make do without that statute. The opposite is also true: If a statute already does exist, then that statute likely will stay on the books throughout the president's term.

Power of the Purse: Congress's Control over the Budget

Congress wields a second major lever of power over the president—one that also involves its ability to enact legislation but that nevertheless warrants its own discussion. This power is often referred to as Congress's power of the purse. This power allows Congress to control, via statute, how the federal government can (and cannot) spend money. The Constitution confers this power by granting spending authority to Congress, which exercises it through the passage of budget-related laws, often called appropriations bills. The Constitution then prohibits the federal government, including the president, from spending money outside of what Congress's statutes have authorized. As a result of this arrangement, a president is very much at the financial mercy of Congress. He normally cannot spend even a cent without congressional authorization.

In order to help Congress figure out what to spend money on, the president can make spending recommendations. Indeed, by statute, Congress actually requires the president to present it with a proposed budget each fiscal year. Yet Congress need not adopt the president's proposals. Ultimately, the legislative branch gets to decide how to appropriate money.

Consider, to this end, President Trump's campaign promise to build a border wall—what he called an "impenetrable, physical, tall, powerful, beautiful, southern" edifice along the United States' border with Mexico.[10] In his first week in office, Trump issued an executive order announcing his intention to build the wall right away. In a televised speech, he reiterated this point: "The Secretary of Homeland Security, working with myself, and my staff, will begin immediate construction."[11]

Trump's plan quickly hit a snag. Weeks after his announcement, the Department of Homeland Security confirmed that it could only locate around $20 million from funds that, by law, could even possibly be used on the project.[12] Yet the projected cost for Trump's wall was in the billions. Not to be deterred, Trump responded on March 16, 2017, by sending a proposed budget to Congress. He called it "America First: A Budget Blueprint to Make America Great Again."[13] This blueprint proposed, among other things, that billions of dollars be allocated for the wall's construction. The budget also made other proposals: that significant funding be cut from the National Institutes of Health, for example, and that the allotment for the Environmental Protection Agency be sliced by nearly a third.

Less than two months later, Congress passed its own budget bill, which Trump quickly signed into law. This final budget bill, which kept the government running and avoided a government shutdown, looked very different from Trump's blueprint. It included, among other things, billions of dollars in *additional* funding for the National Institutes of Health, a mere 1 percent cut in the Environmental Protection Agency's budget, and no money at all for the construction of a new, physical wall on the United States-Mexico border. Just like President Bush back in 1990, Trump had been forced to reach a compromise with Congress. And just like in 1990, that compromise came at the expense of the president's political agenda.

This congressional power over spending affects far more than big-ticket items like a border wall. It affects everything and anything the executive branch wants to spend money on.

Consider the money that the executive branch needs in order to enforce federal drug laws that criminalize marijuana. As of 2017, federal law makes it a crime to manufacture, distribute, or possess marijuana. Marijuana therefore remains illegal across the country—even in Seattle, Washington, where it is advertised on billboards and storefronts, and in Denver, Colorado, where marijuana dispensaries outnumber Starbucks stores.[14] It is even illegal in California, where county health departments have for years been issuing official medical marijuana identification cards. The many state laws purporting to authorize the use of marijuana for medical and recreational purposes do not change the fact that federal laws criminalize the drug. Indeed, these state marijuana laws, in a sense, do nothing more than assure marijuana users within these states that, if they go to jail for mere marijuana use, it will not be for violating *state* law. Rather, it will be for violating *federal* law.

This arrangement creates uncertainty and understandably raises concern for residents of such states. As a result, those affected have pressured the federal government to back away from this area. By 2014, such political pressure prompted Congress to use its power over spending to pass what is known as the Rohrabacher-Farr amendment. This amendment prohibits the federal government from spending any money to prosecute marijuana-related crimes if spending that money would interfere with state efforts to "authorize the use, distribution, possession, or cultivation of medical marijuana."[15] To be clear, the Rohrabacher-Farr amendment did not alter federal laws criminalizing marijuana use.

Instead, by limiting how the federal government can spend money, it significantly undermined the ability of the Department of Justice to prosecute people for marijuana-related federal crimes.[16]

Spending restrictions like those contained in the Rohrabacher-Farr amendment reach all facets of government—even where presidential power is at its highest. In the world of foreign affairs, for example, Congress has used its spending power to push back on the country's involvement in unpopular military conflicts, such as the Vietnam War. Congress also has flexed its spending muscles in response to a related but distinct problem: a president's attempt to impound funds—that is, to refuse to spend money that Congress has allocated. In response to politically controversial impoundments by President Nixon,[17] Congress in 1974 enacted the Impoundment Control Act. This act asserted Congress's control over the practice and gave the president a mechanism by which he could seek congressional approval prior to engaging in it. Coupled with federal court rulings calling into question whether presidents ever have the authority to impound funds contrary to congressional intent,[18] Congress's 1974 statute has cut down on subsequent presidents' use of the practice.

In short, Congress's spending power reaches all aspects of government and operates as a significant check on the president.

"You're Hired!": Congress's Control over Appointments

Congress exercises further control over the president in matters of employment. As we described in chapter 2, the Constitution grants the president the ability to nominate individuals for extremely influential positions in government. Nomination, however, is only the first step. Once an individual has been nominated, she must be confirmed by the Senate. In light of this requirement, the president gets his preferred picks for certain high-level government positions only to the extent that he can convince a majority of senators—each with a separate set of desires and concerns—to vote in favor of his nominees.

Candidates for high-level appointments have their work cut out for them. The process generally begins even before the candidate has been nominated with an intimidating combination of investigations and vetting from the FBI and others. Unsurprisingly, these investigations often reveal snags. For a candidate with complications serious enough to call into question whether the Senate will confirm her, this can be the end of the road.

Once a president is satisfied with what he knows about a candidate and wants to move forward, the Senate begins its own extensive, and often intrusive, vetting. The Senate's process normally includes written questionnaires as well as hearings, viewable by the public, in which senators question the candidate—sometimes nicely, sometimes not. Throughout the proceedings, candidates try to avoid even the slightest error, as misrepresentations might not only inflict political costs but also violate the law.

Armed with the information it needs, the Senate then decides whether to bring the nominee up for a vote. Senators have many ways to delay confirmation votes, and members of the controlling party generally can extend that delay indefinitely.

In 2016, Senate Republicans took this approach in response to President Obama's nominee for the Supreme Court, Judge Merrick Garland. By nearly all accounts, Judge Garland, a federal judge on the U.S. Court of Appeals for the D.C. Circuit, was highly qualified for the position. A graduate of Harvard College and Harvard Law School, Garland had served as a law clerk to a Supreme Court justice, practiced law at a major law firm, and worked as a federal prosecutor, where he played a major role in prosecuting the Oklahoma City bombers. Nonetheless, Republicans in control of the Senate refused to let his nomination proceed. Many months passed without a hearing, much less a vote. By the time Obama left office, Judge Garland's nomination had simply expired. In this way, Republicans were able to aggressively push back against the president without having to formally vote down his nominee.

In 2017, the Republicans in control of the Senate engaged in even more complicated procedural maneuverings, including eliminating the filibuster threat for Supreme Court appointments, in order to ensure that President Trump's nominee, Judge Neil Gorsuch, would receive a vote. (In so doing, Republicans pointed to the precedent set in 2013 by Democrats, who had eliminated the filibuster threat for other presidential nominees.) The plan worked. Republicans were able to confirm Trump's nominee to the same seat that Judge Garland had been nominated to fill.

Besides engaging in procedural maneuvering to thwart a president's nominee, the Senate often can reach the same result in another way: by pressuring nominees to withdraw. In December 2016, President Trump announced that he would nominate Andrew Puzder, the CEO of an enormous fast-food conglomerate, to head the Department of Labor. Criticism quickly followed. Labor groups bemoaned Puzder's outspoken resistance to a minimum-wage increase. Democrats cited allegations of mistreatment lodged against Puzder and his businesses by workers and others. Soon even Republican senators were piling on, accusing Puzder of, among other things, hiring an undocumented woman to serve as his housekeeper. Puzder saw the writing on the wall. Rather than suffer a formal rejection, he withdrew himself from consideration. Withdrawals like these further illustrate the power the Senate wields through confirmation.

Assuming that a candidate sticks it out and the Senate proceeds to a vote, the candidate needs a majority of senators to approve her nomination. At this point, nearly all nominees succeed. It is very rare for the Senate to vote down a nominee who has made it to a final Senate vote. Occasionally, however, the Senate does exactly that—and the result can make history. Judge Robert H. Bork, whose confirmation proceeding has been called "one of the fiercest battles ever waged over a Supreme Court nominee,"[19] gained celebrity (at least among lawyers) based on the dubious honor of triggering a failed Senate vote.

In 1987, President Reagan nominated Bork to the U.S. Supreme Court. At the time, Bork was a federal judge on the U.S. Court of Appeals for the D.C. Circuit. Senator Ted Kennedy, who was particularly incensed by Bork's record on civil rights, responded to the nomination with a diatribe on the Senate floor. His description of "Robert Bork's America" would become famous:

> Robert Bork's America is a land in which women would be forced into back-alley abortions, blacks would sit at segregated lunch counters, rogue police could break down citizens' doors in midnight raids, schoolchildren could not be taught about evolution, writers and artists would be censored at the whim

of government, and the doors of the Federal courts would be shut on the fingers of millions of citizens for whom the judiciary is often the only protector of the individual rights that are the heart of our democracy.[20]

Despite this scathing attack, Bork made it to a full Senate vote. Yet criticism followed him throughout the process, and, in the end, the Senate voted 58–42 to reject his nomination.

Judge Bork's experience, while dramatic, was unusual. Indeed, in over 200 years, the Senate has formally voted down fewer than fifteen nominees to the Supreme Court, out of more than 150 nominations. The Senate has subjected even fewer cabinet-level nominees to such treatment. As of 2017, the most recent cabinet-level nominee to trigger this rare response was John Tower, whose nomination to serve as the secretary of defense under President George H.W. Bush was rejected in 1989 amid allegations of alcohol abuse, misconduct toward women, and conflicts of interest. (Or at least that is how Senate Democrats explained their decision to reject the nomination of their former colleague.) Prior to Tower, the Senate had not voted down any cabinet-level nominee since it rejected President Eisenhower's nomination for secretary of commerce in 1959. Eisenhower's nominee had hit the hard wall of politics, with the Senate purportedly rejecting his candidacy in retaliation for the "high-handed manner" in which the nominee previously had interacted with the senators.[21]

Despite the infrequency of these formal rejections, the Senate exercises enormous control over confirmations. Indeed, the Senate's appointment power is so strong that many presidential picks simply never make it to the final stage.

The Truth, the Whole Truth, and Nothing but the Truth: Congress's Oversight Power

A fourth way Congress exerts control over the executive branch, including the president, is via congressional oversight. Oversight—also referred to as congressional investigation—is a wide-ranging power. Congressional investigations can address any topic on which Congress might choose to regulate. Congress's power of oversight, in other words, "is as penetrating and far-reaching as the potential power to enact [legislation] and appropriate [funds] under the Constitution."[22]

Congressional oversight takes many different forms, including committee hearings, where witnesses are called to testify, and requests to the executive branch for written reports. Oversight also might involve Congress's use of the subpoena, which enables Congress to compel individuals or entities to provide information (through, for example, live testimony or the production of documents). Those who refuse to comply with a congressional subpoena may suffer legal consequences—possibly even jail time.

Some of these forms of congressional oversight flow from the Constitution, others from statutes, and still others from Congress's own rules. Collectively, these legal sources provide Congress with wide authority to investigate many things, including the executive branch. It may come as little surprise, then, that congressional oversight has played a role in some of the most sensational moments in presidential history, including the impeachment and near conviction of President Andrew Johnson in the years after the Civil War, Watergate during the Nixon era, Iran-Contra in the Reagan years, and the Monica Lewinsky scandal that plagued President Clinton.[23]

One reason why congressional oversight stands as such a powerful tool is because Congress need not obtain the president's approval to launch an oversight proceeding. Nor must Congress obtain the consent of both houses of Congress. Indeed, oversight is often conducted by one congressional committee or another, not by Congress as a whole. In this sense, it is much easier for Congress to launch oversight proceedings than it is for Congress to legislate.[24]

In addition to investigating actions taken directly by presidents, congressional oversight proceedings often examine actions taken by high-level executive branch officials who work underneath the president. One particularly notable example of such oversight occurred in 2007 when members of Congress became increasingly frustrated with the Bush Administration's Department of Justice, which at the time was run by Attorney General Alberto Gonzales. The growing frustration with DOJ stemmed from multiple scandals, including one relating to a warrantless domestic eavesdropping program and another relating to allegedly improper firings of high-level federal prosecutors. Members of Congress—trying to figure out what the attorney general had known and done about these matters—hauled Gonzales before House and Senate committees and demanded that he answer pointed questions under oath. When reports later emerged suggesting that Gonzales had been inaccurate in this testimony to Congress, the calls for his resignation reached a fever pitch. On August 27, 2007, in response to pressure from Congress, Gonzales announced he was resigning.

These 2007 hearings received widespread press coverage, which tends to occur whenever Congress's investigations involve allegations of a scandal. Indeed, similarly extensive coverage characterized Congress's investigation into Russia's involvement in the 2016 U.S. presidential election. At times, these sorts of highly publicized investigations can inflict political costs and force the executive's hand.

Most of Congress's oversight work, however, does not involve allegations of scandals and does not receive this same level of attention. For example, members of Congress routinely hold far more mundane—but still extremely important—hearings related to agency budgets. In addition, multiple laws require many of those working within the executive branch to provide periodic reports to Congress, and to supplement these accounts with special reports in response to particularly serious problems. Through these forms of oversight, members of Congress can determine how best to respond—through legislation or some other tool—to developments, whether positive or negative, in the executive branch.

High Crimes and Misdemeanors: Congress's Impeachment Power

Perhaps the most dramatic way Congress exercises control over the president is through the power of impeachment. This power, given to Congress by the Constitution, has two parts: impeachment and conviction. Combined, they give Congress the extraordinary power to oust the president from office. They also allow Congress to remove other high-ranking members of the federal government, including executive branch officials, judges, and justices.

Impeachment proceedings begin in the House of Representatives, which alone has the power to impeach an official, including the president. The House accomplishes this by voting on an article of impeachment, which is a document identifying charges against the official. While the Constitution requires that these charges be for "Treason, Bribery, or other high Crimes and Midemeanors,"[25] the courts have indicated that it is up to Congress, and not the courts themselves, to decide what this language means.

If a majority of the members of the House approve of an article of impeachment, the official has been impeached. In December 1998, for example, President Clinton was impeached when the House of Representatives voted to approve two articles of impeachment against him: one for perjury and the other for obstructing justice.

Impeachment, however, is just the beginning. At that point, the official still has his job, just as before. The Senate then takes up consideration of the impeachment articles, and this proceeds in the style of a trial. If the president is the official who has been impeached, the chief justice of the Supreme Court presides over the proceedings. At the conclusion of the trial, the senators vote on whether to convict the official of the impeachment charges. If two-thirds or more of senators vote to convict, the official is removed from office.

As of 2017, the House of Representatives has impeached a president only twice: once in 1868 in the wake of the Civil War (against President Andrew Johnson, who was alleged to have violated a statute protecting high-level political appointees) and again in 1998 (against President Clinton, who was alleged to have lied under oath about his affair with a White House intern). In neither of those cases was the Senate willing to convict. Clinton escaped conviction because only fifty senators, rather than the sixty-seven needed for a two-thirds majority, voted to convict him for obstruction of justice, and even fewer voted to convict him for perjury. As this record confirms, the impeachment and removal process gives a relatively small number of senators the power to save a president from ouster. This helps to explain why conviction and removal of a president is so elusive.

Congress also has the power, through impeachment and conviction, to remove others in high-ranking government positions. These include members of the federal judiciary and high-level executive officers. Yet

Congress's record in this regard is similarly sparse. As of 2017, Congress has never used its impeachment power to remove an executive branch official or a member of the Supreme Court. In addition, as we noted earlier, out of the thousands of judges who have been appointed to the lower federal courts, Congress has used its impeachment power to remove only eight. Allegations against these eight judges ranged from adjudicating while drunk to waging war against the United States government.

Still, the threat of impeachment always hangs over a president's head, and it has dramatically changed history at least once. In 1974, Congress's apparent willingness to use its impeachment power helped to convince President Richard Nixon to resign in the wake of the Watergate scandal. When Nixon resigned, his vice president, Gerald Ford, became president. The Twenty-Fifth Amendment of the Constitution required the substitution: "In case of the removal of the President from office or of his death or resignation, the Vice President shall become President."[26]

The Twenty-Fifth Amendment also provides for another set of procedures—separate and apart from impeachment procedures—for taking away a president's powers and placing them in the hands of the vice president. These procedures are meant to apply when a president is "unable to discharge the powers and duties of his office."[27] Importantly, it is not the voters or even the courts who decide whether this condition is met. Rather, it is either the president himself or a select list of high-ranking officials. In the first scenario, the president declares himself unable to discharge his powers and duties. In response, the powers and duties fall temporarily to the vice president.

Recent presidents have availed themselves of this option. In 2002, for example, President George W. Bush had to undergo general anesthesia for a routine medical examination, and he invoked the Twenty-Fifth Amendment prior to the procedure. As a result, Vice President Dick Cheney became the acting president of the United States for two hours and fifteen minutes. Bush took nearly identical steps five years later when he underwent the same routine examination.

In the other scenario contemplated by the Twenty-Fifth Amendment, the vice president and select others (either high-ranking cabinet officials or another body designated by Congress) may declare that the president is "unable to discharge the powers and duties of his office."[28] If this occurs, the powers and duties of the presidency drop automatically to the vice president. However, a resistant president has a very good shot at taking those powers right back. All he has to do is contest the conclusion that he suffers from an inability. If the disagreement persists, the dispute gets transferred to Congress. At that point, the president will retain his powers unless Congress, by a two-thirds vote in each house, agrees that he cannot fulfill his obligations.

Never in American history has Congress stripped a president of power through the mechanism set forth in the Twenty-Fifth Amendment. This record is unsurprising in light of all the actors who would need to take a stand against the president. This mechanism requires not only that the president's own vice president seek his ouster, but also that either a congressionally designated body or a majority of his cabinet (hand-selected by the president and subject to termination by the same) decide that his powers should be stripped. Even then, unless the president acquiesces, the procedure is far from complete. A full two-thirds of each house of Congress still must take the unprecedented step of forcibly relieving the president of his duties. In this sense, removing power from the president through the Twenty-Fifth Amendment is even more difficult than doing so through impeachment; it requires buy-in from a far wider range of actors.

Congress may at some point make history by turning to its impeachment power or to its power under the Twenty-Fifth Amendment to force a president's ouster from office. But it would take something akin to a perfect political storm. As of 2017, that storm has yet to hit the United States.

In Sum: Congress Has Many Levers of Control over the President

Congress has a number of significant points of leverage over a president, including those associated with the power of legislation, appropriations, appointment, oversight, and impeachment. As a result, if Congress fails to exercise its authority to control the president, it is likely for reasons that are political rather than legal.

This reference to politics leads to a related point: The more power that these legal levers provide Congress over the president, the more control each civic participant has over the president. This is because members of Congress generally do try to listen to constituents and respond to their concerns. In the power struggles between Congress and the president, political pressure can make a difference.

In short, our country's system of checks and balances allows Congress to play a central role. Still, as the next chapter will explain, the legislative branch is far from alone in providing a check on the president. Indeed, pushback can come from within the executive branch itself.

CHAPTER 5

How the Executive Branch Checks the President

Being president is a lot like being superintendent of a big cemetery: There's a lot of people under you, and nobody is listening.

— Bill Clinton speaking in 2014 about his tenure as president[1]

Every branch of the U.S. government can check a president's power. Even the executive branch—consisting of an enormous workforce of millions of people—can assist, derail, or otherwise affect the agenda of its chief executive. As this chapter explains, the influence of these federal employees derives in part from the laws that empower and protect them in their work.

The Nature of the Federal Executive Branch

The executive branch of the federal government employs approximately two million civilian workers.[2] Unsurprisingly, therefore, proponents of smaller government frequently call for its reform. For example, in 2011, Rick Perry, the then-governor of Texas, advocated this position while running to become the Republican nominee for the 2012 presidential election. Taking the stage for a televised debate, Perry hoped to make clear that he was a serious contender in the fight for a more limited government. Instead, what Perry made clear was that the executive branch is so vast and complicated that it often is difficult to keep it straight.

During the debate, Perry forcefully held up three fingers while announcing that he would ax "three agencies" from the executive branch. Perry then froze when trying to remember their names. "It's three agencies of government, when I get there, that are gone—commerce, education, and the, um, what's the third one there? Let's see," Perry stumbled.

The crowd laughed awkwardly, prompting the debate moderator to ask, incredulously, "But you can't name the third one?"

Perry tried, but came up short again. "The third agency of government I would do away with—the education, uh, the, uh, commerce and let's see. I can't—the third one, I can't. Sorry. Oops." Later, Perry made clear that the Department of Energy was the agency whose name had escaped him.[3]

Although this slip-up doomed Perry's 2012 presidential bid, it did not kill his long-term career prospects. Far from it. In 2017, President Trump nominated, and the Senate approved, Perry to serve as the head of the Department of Energy—the very same agency Perry had threatened to eliminate. This means that Perry was charged with running a federal agency with an annual budget of more than $25 billion and that employs more than 14,000 government workers, plus approximately 90,000 contractors.[4] These employees and contractors work in various labs, offices, and programs within the agency. These include the Office of Nuclear Energy, the Office of Fossil Energy, the Office of Energy Efficiency and Renewable Energy, and the Office of Science.[5]

Despite its large size and scope, the Department of Energy is just one agency among many in the executive branch—by some counts, there are more than 100.[6] Together, these agencies constitute the means by which presidents implement and enforce statutes that affect all facets of American life, whether relating to agriculture, the environment, or education; immigration, financial markets, or labor; taxes, telecommunications, or military operations; and so on.

Keeping track of all these executive branch agencies is no easy task. At the most basic level, it requires familiarizing oneself with the official names of these agencies and their common acronyms. The Federal Communications Commission, for example, is commonly referred to as the FCC. It is responsible for administering and enforcing the nation's communications laws and regulations. The Department of Homeland Security, which is called DHS, implements and enforces various laws that protect the nation from threats, such as those involving border security, transportation security, and emergency management. The Public Company Accounting Oversight Board is nicknamed "Peekaboo" (perhaps because PCAOB is too much of a mouthful). It oversees and regulates entities that audit public companies.

Further complicating matters is the fact that many agencies consist of a dizzying array of subcomponents, often referred to as offices and bureaus. These subparts, in turn, have their own nicknames. In the end, what emerges is a veritable alphabet soup filled with so many different flavors and varieties that it is hard not to become overwhelmed by the complexity of it all.

A president, however, needs to find some way to keep it straight. As soon as his term begins, he is immediately responsible for overseeing the multitude of agencies, officers, and employees that make up the executive branch. For a president to move his agenda forward, he needs the cooperation of this vast executive branch machinery.

Some individuals who work within the executive branch listen carefully to the president. Others do not. As this chapter describes, the members of the executive branch most likely to follow a president's directions are political appointees. The president selects these appointees and is free to fire many of them. By contrast, career executive branch employees are less likely to jump whenever the president demands it. Members of this latter group are insulated from politics, and they tend not to be indebted to any one administration or political party.

Political Appointees: The President's Most Loyal Supporters

Political appointees working within the executive branch are generally handpicked by a president or others in his administration. A president picks these individuals precisely because he expects that they will be loyal and help him implement his policy goals.

In 2011, a member of President Obama's administration engaged in an illustrative display of such loyalty. That year, the EPA had been preparing to finalize a rule limiting smog, an air pollutant that can cause asthma and other serious respiratory conditions. The EPA had already held public hearings and gathered public comments, and it sent a draft of its proposed final rule to the White House for review. In response, Obama requested a meeting with Lisa Jackson, the head of the EPA. During their closed-door meeting, the president told Jackson that the EPA should not move forward with its proposed smog standard. Obama explained that the EPA would have an opportunity to revisit the standard, perhaps in 2013, if he were reelected to a second term. But because the smog standards might be politically unpopular in states that were crucial to his reelection campaign, Obama insisted that the EPA hold off.[7] Jackson, a political appointee who worked at the pleasure of the president, reportedly considered resigning under protest. Instead, she complied with Obama's instructions and withdrew the EPA's proposed rule.[8] In other words, she chose to remain loyal to the president.

Jackson's response was typical for political appointees—so much so that deviations from this pattern tend to make headlines. One such incident became known as the Saturday Night Massacre. It unfolded on Saturday, October 20, 1973, in the midst of the Watergate scandal consuming Nixon's presidency. On that day, President Richard Nixon ordered his attorney general—the first in the chain of command within the Department of Justice—to fire Archibald Cox, the special prosecutor in charge of investigating Watergate-related crimes. Yet the attorney general refused to comply. Instead, he resigned. Undeterred, Nixon ordered the second-in-command at DOJ to fire the special prosecutor. Yet that official also refused to comply with the president's order and instead resigned. Eventually the third in the chain of command complied with Nixon's order and fired Cox. As a legal matter, this termination resulted in the end of Cox's tenure as special prosecutor. In addition, as a political matter, it triggered a firestorm. In one day, Nixon's orders had taken out two of the nation's most powerful law-enforcement officers, as well as the special prosecutor investigating possible criminal activity involving high-level executive branch officials. Members of Congress, the media, and the American public all took notice, and the calls for Nixon's impeachment grew dramatically louder.

A more recent example of pushback by a political appointee emerged early in Trump's presidency. In January 2017, Trump nominated Rod Rosenstein to serve as the deputy attorney general, the second-in-command at DOJ. In April, the Senate confirmed Rosenstein to this position. Less than a month later, Rosenstein did something that Trump previously had insisted was neither necessary nor appropriate: He appointed a special counsel to investigate "any links and/or coordination between the Russian government and individuals associated with the campaign of President Donald Trump."[9] Rosenstein did so by relying upon regulations that DOJ had adopted in 1999. Pursuant to these pre-existing regulations, a special counsel is an individual, hired from outside the government, who is tasked with conducting an independent investigation into a matter that DOJ cannot itself properly investigate.

Trump was not pleased. He denounced the decision on Twitter, referring to the proceedings as "the single greatest witch hunt of a politician in American history!"[10] Despite his frustration, Trump had limited options. DOJ's regulations expressly limited the circumstances under which the special counsel could be fired—and, in any event, the regulations placed the authority to fire the special counsel with Rosenstein, not Trump. As a result, the law did not give Trump a clear means by which to fire the special counsel. In addition, firing Rosenstein (while legally within Trump's powers) would have fanned the flames of political controversy already swirling around the Russian meddling allegations. As a result, Trump's initial reaction was to quite begrudgingly accept the appointment of the special counsel.

Despite these precedents, it is rare for political appointees to make decisions that run so contrary to a president's preferences. When a political appointee nevertheless pushes back, the president may pressure that official to resign—or serve that official with a termination notice.

Civil Servants: Their Loyalties Lie Elsewhere

Although political appointees often cooperate with a president's requests, only a very small percentage of the individuals working as employees within the executive branch are political appointees. In fact, more than two million civilians working in the executive branch are career civil servants.[11] Thanks to statutes enacted by Congress, these civil servants generally obtain their jobs through a merit-based system, not a system of political spoils.[12] Once hired, these employees are subject to federal laws that restrict them in some ways and protect them in others.

On the one hand, federal law prohibits career civil servants from engaging in many partisan political activities. These employees generally may not, for example, serve as candidates in partisan elections, engage in political activities while at work, or try to pressure their subordinates into political activity.[13] On the other hand, federal law generally protects these same civil servants from being fired or demoted for political reasons.[14] As a result of this overlapping set of rules, civil servants tend to stay above the political fray and remain in their jobs, even while presidents and their political appointees come and go.[15] This continuity helps to maintain stability in government. It also means that civil servants' loyalties tend not to lie with any one presidential administration. Rather, civil servants, who may be trained scientists, doctors, engineers, or lawyers, often care more about remaining loyal to the obligations of their profession and to their specific governmental position than to whichever politician may be occupying the Oval Office on a given day.[16]

For all these reasons, civil servants sometimes prove to be a serious thorn in the president's side. If a president's policy goals or preferred positions run contrary to scientific evidence, for example, or if they lack sound policy justifications, civil servants may well try to push back. Doing so can be difficult, but a number of tools of resistance do exist. Some are quite informal.[17] Imagine that the president directs the EPA to consider undoing a particular environmental rule. If civil servants within the EPA prefer the rule as it stands, they might engage in intentional foot dragging—taking their sweet time to study the issue inside and out and then back again, before deciding it is time to take any sort of tangible action.

These sorts of informal tools of resistance raise tricky legal and moral questions. There may, however, be other options available to civil servants who feel compelled to stand up against a president's agenda—options that have more grounding in the law. Two of the most important of these more formal tools involve building a record and blowing the whistle.[18]

Building a Record

Civil servants can, on occasion, push back against the president through the compilation of detailed factual records. By working hard to create expert-driven records filled with factual findings, science, and data, career employees within agencies can make it harder for political appointees to act contrary to the conclusions set forth in those same records. This is because courts generally are more skeptical of agency decisions that run counter to findings made by career staff.[19]

A striking example of this phenomenon emerged in 2009, when a federal judge reviewed the way the FDA handled Plan B, an emergency contraceptive (also known as the morning-after pill) that can reduce the risk of an unwanted pregnancy if a woman takes it soon after having unprotected sex. In 1999, while President Clinton was in office, the FDA approved Plan B for prescription-only use in the United States. Two years later (with President Bush then in office), various organizations asked the FDA to switch Plan B from prescription-only status to over-the-counter status. Studying this issue, scientific staff at the FDA concluded that the benefits of over-the-counter status outweighed any risks, even for adolescents. As a result, the staff recommended making Plan B accessible over the counter, without any age restriction.[20]

Yet not everyone liked the idea of making Plan B accessible to young women and girls. It was not the sort of change supported by President Bush or the officials he had appointed. Some pro-life and religious groups also opposed it. As a result, the political appointees at the FDA dragged their feet in response to the staff recommendation, layering delay on delay. This prompted civil servants at the FDA to grow frustrated.

Senators Hillary Clinton and Patty Murray also became exasperated. In response, the senators placed what is called a hold on one of Bush's nominations, a veterinarian named Lester Crawford whom Bush had tapped to head the FDA. The senators released their hold—thereby allowing Crawford to move through the confirmation process—only after Crawford promised that, under his supervision, the FDA would be allowed to move forward on the Plan B proposal. As a result of Crawford's promise, the Senate finally voted on Crawford's nomination, and he was confirmed.

Immediately after taking office, however, Crawford went back on his promise. In response, a career appointee within the FDA, Dr. Susan Wood, resigned in protest. "Sadly, your recent decision to not approve Plan B emergency contraception, overturning the clear scientific and clinical evidence, contradicts both the FDA mission and my commitment to women's health,"[21] Dr. Wood stated in her resignation letter.

Eventually, in 2006, the FDA announced that it would approve Plan B for over-the-counter status, but only for women eighteen years and older. While some observers approved of the age-based cutoff, others responded with exasperation—and they called their lawyers. In response to a lawsuit that followed, a federal judge concluded that undue political pressure had indeed tainted the FDA's decision to impose the age restriction. In reaching this conclusion, the judge took particular note of push-back by career employees at the FDA—that is, of the conclusions reached by the FDA's scientific staff and of Dr. Wood's resignation. In short, civil servants' efforts to build a factual record had worked. The record helped to convince a federal judge to invalidate the FDA's decision and send the matter back to the FDA for reconsideration.[22]

All this helps to show the power that career employees can have on an executive branch activity. Through diligent work and the creation of an evidentiary record, civil servants occasionally can push back against excessive pressure by political appointees.

Blowing the Whistle

Another tool available to concerned civil servants involves disclosure. When a civil servant witnesses wrongdoing by the government, she faces a series of difficult choices, including whether to stay silent or to go public. When an employee opts for the latter—for revealing information about illegal or dangerous government activity—it is called whistleblowing. A civil servant's decision to blow the whistle can have momentous consequences for a president, and for the whistleblower.

Whistleblowers played a crucial role in the downfall of President Nixon. In the early 1970s, one of the most famous whistleblowers in U.S. history, Daniel Ellsberg, leaked the so-called Pentagon Papers to the *New York Times* and the *Washington Post*. These papers demonstrated that the U.S. government had deceived the American people about the war in Vietnam. For many, this revelation provoked outrage. In response to Ellsberg's decision to leak the papers, the Nixon-run White House ordered a unit, called "the plumbers," to break into the office of Ellsberg's psychologist and seek notes of the psychologist's sessions with Ellsberg. This break-in, along with other events from the Watergate era, eventually led to Nixon's resignation—a series of events that vividly illustrates the potential ripple effects of an individual's decision to blow the whistle.[23]

In 1978, Congress responded to these events by providing limit-ed whistleblower protections for civil servants. Later it passed an even stronger measure called the Whistleblower Protection Act. While this Act contains many exceptions, it does provide significant protection to federal whistleblowers who reveal information about violations of the law, as well as information concerning "a substantial and specific danger to public health or safety."[24]

Even though the Whistleblower Protection Act provides real pro-tections, a government employee's decision to expose problems still may come at a high cost. Consider the story of a federal air marshal named Robert J. MacLean. In 2001, MacLean joined the Transportation Security Administration (TSA). His job as an air marshal required him to fly on passenger flights to protect people against potential terrorist attacks. In July 2003, MacLean learned that the TSA was canceling certain air-marshal assignments, despite its instruction that all marshals remain on heightened alert. MacLean believed that this cancellation was both dangerous and illegal, and he unsuccessfully tried to push back through internal government channels. Frustrated with the responses he received, he turned to the media, and MSNBC ran an exposé. As a result of this reporting, the TSA's actions quickly became a national scandal. Within twenty-four hours, members of Congress had become involved, and the TSA had put air marshals back on the flights.

When the TSA later discovered that MacLean was the source of the MSNBC report, it fired him. The agency alleged that MacLean had disclosed "sensitive security information" without authorization. In response, MacLean argued that he was entitled to the protections of the Whistleblower Protection Act. Although it took the former marshal nearly a decade of fighting over these issues, the U.S. Supreme Court eventually sided with MacLean.[25]

The Supreme Court's ruling helped to vindicate MacLean's cause. Still, whistleblowing had inflicted major costs. During the decade it took MacLean to clear his name, he was unable to find any other law-enforce-ment job. One rejection letter he received from a county sheriff's depart-ment particularly stung. Using all caps for emphasis, the letter stated that he could not be hired "due to issues involving INTEGRITY."[26]

Many employees who try to petition the courts for protection under the federal whistleblower law fare even worse than MacLean, given that such lawsuits frequently do not succeed.[27] Even more dramatically, the unauthorized disclosure of governmental information can in rare cases land an individual in jail, a topic we will come back to in chapter 8.

While whistleblowing therefore remains an important source of power for civil servants, it is one that provides incomplete legal protection. Executive branch employees who decide to disclose details about illegal or dangerous actions taking place within the executive branch may, at times, help to protect the public against improper conduct by the president or those working beneath him. Yet this decision often comes at the whistleblower's own expense.

In Sum: Government Workers Can Help or Hinder the President

The executive branch is a complex and vast machinery with millions of employees. If the president wants to get anything done, he needs to harness the power of these many individuals, who may or may not be enthusiastic about his agenda. Political appointees generally are eager to help the president in these efforts. Career civil servants, by contrast, may not be quite so cooperative. This is due, at least in part, to various legal rules that help to set the balance of power among the president and the many officers and employees working under his supervision.

As confirmed by the case of Robert MacLean, part of that balance of power involves the courts and their ability to check executive overreach. We turn now to this third branch of government: the federal judiciary.

CHAPTER 6

How Courts Check the President

Whenever you put a man on the Supreme Court, he ceases to be your friend, you can be sure of that.

— President Harry S. Truman speaking to a group of students in 1959[1]

A wave of lawsuits swept through the White House in President Trump's early days in office. These lawsuits attacked all sorts of things—early executive orders, conflicts of interest posed by Trump's business dealings, allegedly defamatory statements Trump made before becoming president, and more. Never before had a president faced such a sudden and forceful influx of litigation. All these lawsuits necessarily pulled another branch of government into the fray: the judicial branch.

The result was a striking display of judicial power that unfolded in the first 100 days of Trump's presidency. During this short window of time, lower federal court judges temporarily blocked not one, not two, but *three* of Trump's early executive orders.[2] To understand the significance of such a development, consider that collectively U.S. presidents have issued thousands of executive orders. Yet from the birth of the nation up through the end of Obama's presidency, federal courts have blocked only a small handful.[3] This record helps to put into perspective the clash—unprecedented in its speed and scope—between President Trump and the courts.

The first two of Trump's blocked orders involved his travel bans. As we discussed in this book's early pages, the president issued these orders in an effort to restrict travel by citizens of various majority Muslim countries. In an attempt to defend the legality of these orders, Trump argued that his constitutional powers, as well as a particular provision found in a congressional statute (called the Immigration and Nationality Act), gave him the authority to impose the travel bans. In response, however, several federal courts concluded in early judicial rulings that these orders likely violated statutory or constitutional restraints, including those contained in the Constitution's Establishment Clause, which prohibits the government from favoring one religion over another.[4]

The other early executive order that the judiciary quickly put on hold involved Trump's threats to cut off federal funding from so-called "sanctuary jurisdictions"—cities and counties that refuse in some way to cooperate with federal efforts to enforce federal immigration laws. A federal district court judge in California temporarily froze this order on the ground that it likely violated various constitutional limits. For example, the judge reasoned that the president's order attempted to place new restrictions on cities' and counties' receipt of federal funds. This was not legally allowable, the judge ruled, because the Constitution expressly gives Congress, not the president, power over the nation's wallet.[5]

It is true that all these rulings in Trump's first 100 days were preliminary and that each was subject to being overturned on appeal. Still, by putting several of Trump's orders on hold in just his first few months, the judicial branch forcefully demonstrated its willingness to intervene when it determines that a president likely has crossed legal lines.

A Hierarchy of Lifetime Appointments: An Overview of the Judicial Branch

The federal judicial branch consists of three levels of courts. At the base of this court system are district courts, which serve as the entry point for most cases in the federal system. These courts, which operate as trial courts, hear both criminal cases (such as federal criminal prosecutions for drug trafficking or money laundering) and civil cases (such as copyright disputes or challenges to the constitutionality of federal laws). In all, there are around ninety district courts spread across the country. Normally, each of these courts has more than one district court judge working in it. Some have over twenty.

Circuit courts sit one rung above district courts in the judicial

hierarchy. Circuit courts (also known as courts of appeals) primarily review challenges to rulings issued by district court judges. Circuit courts
do not hold trials or hear witness testimony, like the district courts
do. Instead, relying on written briefs and oral arguments presented by
lawyers, circuit courts spend most of their time reviewing district court
rulings for errors. When they engage in this review, the circuit courts
normally sit in three-judge panels. Collectively, the three circuit-court
judges review a district court's rulings and decide whether to uphold or
reverse those rulings.

The United States has thirteen circuit courts. Twelve cover a specific
geographic zone of the country. For example, the U.S. Court of Appeals
for the Ninth Circuit covers nine states and two territories, including
Alaska, Arizona, California, Hawaii, Idaho, Montana, Nevada, Oregon,
and Washington, as well as Guam and the Northern Mariana Islands.
It is by far the largest circuit court in the country. Other circuit courts
cover a much smaller geographic territory. The U.S. Court of Appeals for
the District of Columbia Circuit, in particular, only covers Washington,
D.C. Still, it serves as a particularly important court due in part to congressional statutes that direct many important cases its way.

Finally, at the very top of the judicial hierarchy sits the U.S.
Supreme Court. While those who sit on federal district courts and the
circuit courts are called judges, members of the Supreme Court are
referred to as justices. The Supreme Court's main function is to review
decisions that have been issued by lower court judges, including the
federal courts of appeals. Congress has given the Supreme Court the
power to refuse to hear most of the cases that litigants ask it to review, and
every year the Supreme Court refuses many more cases than it agrees to
hear. In fact, in recent years, the Supreme Court has agreed to hear only
about seventy to eighty cases out of the approximately 7,000 requests for
review filed each year. These requests for review, in turn, emerge out of
only a tiny fraction of the hundreds of thousands of cases heard by the
lower federal district and circuit courts, as well as the vast multitude of
additional cases heard by other courts around the country.

Generally, the Supreme Court will agree to hear a case only if
at least four of the court's nine members believe that the case raises
important legal issues. In practice, this is a very high bar. As a result,

the circuit courts effectively operate as the last layer of judicial review in almost all federal court cases.

The Constitution gives Congress the power to control how many federal judgeships there will be in the country. As of 2017, Congress has authorized over 650 district court judgeships and approximately 180 circuit court judgeships in the judicial branch, as well as exactly nine seats for justices on the Supreme Court. That adds up to about 850 people who serve in these important judicial positions and who collectively make up the judicial branch of the United States. Lawyers often refer to these individuals as Article III judges, reflecting the article of the Constitution that creates the judicial branch. These Article III judges constitute a small fraction of the total number of people who work in some capacity or another as judges in the United States. It does not include magistrate judges, for example, who work within the judicial branch under the supervision of Article III judges. Nor does it include judges, such as administrative law judges, who work within the executive branch and who help the federal government decide a variety of matters (such as whether to grant environmental permits, dispense government benefits, or sanction individuals for violating federal securities laws). It also does not include the many judges working for state and local governments. Yet despite its relatively small size, the core group of Article III federal judges is immensely important.

As we mentioned in chapter 4, the Constitution sets the rules of selection for these federal judges. It gives the president the power to nominate his preferred judicial candidate, and the Senate the power to approve or deny the president's pick. Notwithstanding the political land mines associated with Senate confirmation, each president succeeds in pushing a number of his judicial nominees through the process and onto the federal courts.[6] President Obama, for example, convinced the Senate to confirm more than 300 Article III judges. As a result, when Obama left office in January 2017, his appointees filled more than one-third of all the Senate-confirmed seats on the federal bench. Still, there were more than 100 federal court vacancies left to be filled. In 2017, President Trump started the work of filling these vacancies and waited for more seats to open.

Presidents generally try to pick judicial nominees with legal views similar to their own. In practice, this might translate into views about how broadly to apply the Constitution's protections of individual rights, whether to protect states' rights more or less aggressively, and which interpretive approaches to use when analyzing statutes.

Sometimes presidents try to select judicial nominees with particular views of particular cases. On the campaign trail, for example, President Trump suggested he would appoint judges who would overturn *Roe v. Wade*, a key Supreme Court case that protects a woman's right to choose an abortion. At the same time, he implied that he might be willing to appoint judges who would abide by *Obergefell v. Hodges*, a Supreme Court case that guarantees same-sex couples the right to marry.[7]

The reality, however, is that no president—President Trump or otherwise—can guarantee that his appointees will interpret the law exactly as he wants. Once a nominee becomes a federal judge, the president cannot force that judge to overrule one case or to uphold another. This is by constitutional design. As we have discussed, the Constitution gives lifetime tenure to federal judges, with impeachment by Congress serving as the only possible route for forced ouster.[8] In addition, the Constitution insists that federal judges' salaries cannot be decreased while they are in office. This means that all Article III judges—whether they are district court judges, circuit court judges, or Supreme Court justices—effectively hold their jobs, at a set minimum salary, for life.

As we discussed in chapter 1, state court judges do not necessarily receive the same protections. This is because each state has its own court system that operates separately from the federal judicial system. Although the U.S. Constitution mandates that *federal* judges be given lifetime tenure and salary protections, it says nothing of what protections *states* must provide to their own judges or how state court judges must be selected in the first place.

Job security also varies among the many judges, employed by the federal government, called non-Article III judges. These judges, such as the magistrate judges and administrative law judges discussed above, either operate within the executive branch or assist Article III judges within the judicial branch. Courts have read the Constitution to give Congress flexibility in deciding what types of protections these judges will receive. The Constitution requires only that the small, select group of Article III federal judges who collectively make up the judicial branch receive lifetime tenure and salary protections.

These constitutional protections help to explain why the judicial branch is sometimes referred to as an independent branch, one that is not political in the same way that the executive or legislative branches are. It also helps to explain why President Trump—as upset as he was about the judges' rulings regarding some of his early executive orders—was not able to fire those judges but instead felt compelled to appeal their rulings to higher-level courts.

A Delicate Balance: Federal Court Review of Presidential Power

The drafters of the Constitution expected members of the executive and the legislative branches to be influenced by policy preferences and the political winds. Not so for the judicial branch. Instead, federal judges are supposed to base their rulings on the law.

To help ensure that judges do not unnecessarily entangle themselves in political disputes or abstract controversies, the Constitution empowers federal judges to hear only certain types of cases. At the outset, the Constitution empowers courts to hear only real, live disputes between opposing parties. A federal judge cannot simply read about some presidential action in the newspaper while drinking her morning coffee and then dash off an opinion setting forth her views on the legality (or the illegality) of the action. Instead, judges must wait for an actual case to be brought to the courts by a harmed party.

The Supreme Court made this clear as early as 1793, when it rejected an overture made by President Washington. Washington had wanted the Supreme Court to provide answers to legal questions that his administration had been grappling with in response to a brewing crisis in Europe. In response to a request for guidance sent by Washington's administration, the Supreme Court politely—but flatly—refused. In a letter it sent back to Washington, the court explained that it would be improper for the court to provide anyone, even the president, with general legal advice outside the context of a particular case. It emphasized the need for each branch of government to comply with constitutional limits and avoid overstepping its authority. "The Lines of Separation drawn by the Constitution between the three Departments of Government—their being in certain Respects checks on each other—and our being Judges of a court in the last Resort—are Considerations which afford strong arguments against the Propriety of our extrajudicially deciding the questions alluded to,"[9] the court explained in its letter. Its tone then turned almost contrite.

"We exceedingly regret every Event that may cause Embarrassment to your administration," the letter read. "But we derive Consolation from the Reflection, that your Judgment will discern what is Right, and that your usual Prudence, Decision and Firmness will surmount every obstacle to the Preservation of the Rights, Peace, and Dignity of the [U]nited States."[10]

Despite the kind language, the court had made its answer clear: Outside of a live, concrete case brought to it by an injured party, it would not offer its legal opinions.

These sorts of limits on the judicial power help to explain why so many unresolved questions continue to swirl around the limits of a president's authority. For purposes of illustration, consider one particularly difficult question of presidential power: the legality of presidents' decisions to commit U.S. troops to military actions abroad without clear congressional approval. When faced with lawsuits turning on this question, the federal courts generally have refused to weigh in. In many of these cases, the courts have reasoned that the individuals filing the lawsuits have not suffered a concrete, individualized harm. This occurred in 2016 when a U.S. Army captain brought suit against President Obama. Challenging a military campaign against ISIS (called Operation Inherent Resolve), the captain argued that the campaign was illegal because, based on his reading of the relevant statutes, Congress had not authorized it. Yet the captain did not claim that he personally had incurred (or even feared he would incur) a physical injury associated with the president's orders. Nor did he claim that he wished not to fight. To the contrary, the captain acknowledged that he actually supported the military effort—having concluded that the hostilities against ISIS were "justified both militarily and morally."[11] The captain nevertheless brought the lawsuit because he feared that, by supporting a military effort that might be illegal, he was violating his oath to "preserve, protect, and defend the Constitution of the United States."[12]

In response, a federal district court refused to consider the legality of Operation Inherent Resolve. Instead, it concluded that the army captain had failed to identify a concrete interest, particular to him, sufficient to enable the courts to hear the lawsuit.[13] In legal terms, this is referred to as a lack of standing to sue. Without standing, no lawsuit can go forward in federal court.

Even if a challenger can overcome standing rules, the federal courts still may be unwilling to hear a lawsuit. This is because the federal courts also have declined to resolve cases that, at their core, raise *political* rather than *legal* questions. (Often, this principle is referred to as the limitation posed by the "political question doctrine.") This principle helps to explain, for example, why the Supreme Court refused to decide a controversial case that Senator Barry Goldwater and other members of Congress brought in the 1970s. President Jimmy Carter had nullified a defense treaty with Taiwan without asking for congressional approval. According to the challengers, the Constitution does not give the president the legal power to nullify treaties all on his own. This lawsuit initially produced conflicting opinions among the lower courts. But then the U.S. Supreme Court concluded that it would not allow the case to go forward. Although the justices were not unanimous in how they approached the case, four members of the Supreme Court concluded that the case turned on questions that were for the political branches to answer, not for the courts.[14] The court, as a result, dismissed the case without deciding the merits of the challengers' claims.[15]

Limits like these significantly constrain the judiciary's power. Still, don't be misled: There remain plenty of disputes involving presidential power, and many more involving politics in one way or another, that the federal courts can and do resolve. *Bush v. Gore*, a politically explosive case in which the Supreme Court weighed in on a dispute surrounding the 2000 presidential election, provides just one such example.[16] Though that case involved politically contentious issues, high-profile controversy was not enough to deter the Supreme Court. Generally, so long as the courts determine that a case presents questions of law, and so long as challengers with standing have framed their claims appropriately, the courts can weigh in.

When the courts agree to decide a case, a wide range of issues may be implicated. Cases testing the limits of presidential power can be grouped loosely into the following four buckets: judicial review of *legislation*; judicial review of *official presidential action*, such as executive orders; judicial review of action taken by executive branch *agencies*; and judicial review of actions taken by the president in his *personal capacity*. Each of these presents different legal issues for the courts to consider.

Cases Challenging the Constitutionality of Legislation

The courts are sometimes asked to review the constitutionality of legislation enacted by Congress, including legislation supported and signed into law by the president. When asked to adjudicate such a challenge, the courts take their job extremely seriously. Yet the courts usually will conclude that the legislation is constitutional.

Consider again the Affordable Care Act—the far-reaching and politically controversial law that Obama ushered through Congress in 2010. Critics of the law brought suit, arguing that Congress lacked the power to force individuals to purchase health care. Yet when the case eventually reached the Supreme Court, a majority of the court upheld most of the statute.

In reaching its decision, Chief Justice John Roberts explained the court's reluctance to "invalidate the acts of the Nation's elected leaders."[17] According to the chief justice, members of the judiciary are given only "the authority to interpret the law," not the authority to make policy judgments.[18] Policy determinations are "entrusted to our Nation's elected leaders" precisely because they, unlike federal judges, "can be thrown out of office if the people disagree with them."[19] As a result, when the judicial branch is asked to review the legality of legislation, all a court is supposed to do is ensure that Congress has stayed within the bounds of its legal authority.

Despite the judiciary's generally deferential attitude toward legislative acts, the judiciary sometimes will declare laws to be unconstitutional—even laws that had the full support of the president. The earliest example came way back in 1803, when the Supreme Court decided a case called *Marbury v. Madison*.[22] In this case—a law-school classic—the Supreme Court partially invalidated one of the first statutes ever passed by Congress.

In that case, a man named William Marbury challenged the

refusal of President Thomas Jefferson's staff to deliver a document (called a commission) that would have appointed Marbury to a government job. The commission had been signed and sealed by the administration of the prior president, John Adams. Yet Adams's staff inadvertently had failed to deliver the commission to Marbury in the chaotic final few hours of Adams's presidency. Given the political acrimony between the outgoing and incoming presidents, it seemed clear to Marbury that he was not going to get the commission unless he found some way to force the newly empowered Jefferson Administration to deliver it.

Relying on a law signed by President Washington in 1789, Marbury skipped the lower courts and went straight to the U.S. Supreme Court, asking it to order the new Jefferson Administration to deliver the commission. This put Chief Justice John Marshall (himself appointed to the court by outgoing President Adams) in a tough position: If the court ordered the Jefferson Administration to deliver the commission, the administration might very well thumb its nose at the court, thereby calling into question whether the judiciary really has the final say in what the law required. So, in what is widely viewed as a brilliant strategic move, Chief Justice Marshall issued an opinion that rebuked the Jefferson Administration for illegally withholding the commission but stopped short of ordering the administration to actually deliver it. The chief justice did this by concluding, in the end, that the court simply lacked the power to decide the case. Under his theory, the 1789 law that purported to give Marbury the right to go straight to the Supreme Court (without going first to a lower federal court) was unconstitutional, in light of a technical provision in the Constitution relating to the Supreme Court's power to hear cases.

In ruling this way, Chief Justice Marshall handed the Jefferson Administration a short-term win in this particular case and thereby avoided a showdown between the court and the president. Yet the chief justice's ruling handed an even bigger longer-term win to the courts. It set a precedent whereby the *judiciary* is the branch with the ultimate power to determine the constitutionality of both legislative and executive acts. Indeed, since *Marbury* was issued in 1803, it has been generally accepted in our country that the judicial branch has the power, in the course of deciding such cases, "to say what the law is."[21] This power—to be the authority ultimately to determine what the law means and how it applies in specific challenges, even when those challenges are brought against the government itself—provides the judicial branch with an immensely important means of checking the legality of government action. In short, *Marbury* helped to establish the federal courts' status as a powerful, coequal branch of government.

Marbury also helps to demonstrate how politically motivated decision-making can influence legal outcomes—even within the judicial branch, which supposedly is insulated from politics. Tellingly, however, even the court in *Marbury* felt constrained by legal principles in reaching its decision, and it explained its reasoning in purely legal terms.

More modern examples of the Supreme Court overturning signature pieces of legislation can be found during the New Deal era. During that period, the Supreme Court struck down parts of several pieces of legislation, such as the National Industrial Recovery Act, that President Roosevelt viewed as key to his efforts to jump-start the economy in the wake of the Great Depression. President Roosevelt soon became so frustrated by the court's rulings that he tried to fight back. He even went so far as to propose legislation (never enacted by Congress) that would have greatly increased the number of justices on the Supreme Court. Through his power of nomination, President Roosevelt figured he could pack the court with additional justices, all sharing his views about the constitutionality of his preferred statutes.

Much more recently, the Supreme Court struck down parts of the Brady Handgun Violence Prevention Act.[22] The law was named after James Brady, President Reagan's White House press secretary who was shot during an attempted assassination of Reagan in 1981. President Clinton, who had promised to support gun control while campaigning for the White House, signed the Brady Act into law in 1993. He did so in the presence of Brady himself, who was confined to a wheelchair due to the permanent disabilities he had suffered from the gunshot wound. When the legality of the Brady Act reached the Supreme Court, the court struck down parts of the law that required local law-enforcement officials to help the federal government carry out background checks for gun purchases. According to the court, the Constitution requires the federal government in this circumstance to use its own federal officials to carry out federal law; it cannot force state and local officials to do so on its behalf.

Additional statutes recently held to be unconstitutional, at least in part, include the Voting Rights Act of 1965 (a law protecting the voting rights of racial minorities),[23] the Military Commissions Act of 2006 (a law governing how prisoners in Guantánamo Bay can petition the courts),[24] and the Stolen Valor Act of 2005 (a law criminalizing false claims of having received military honors).[25] According to a 2016 study, the U.S. Supreme Court has declared approximately 180 congressional statutes to be unconstitutional, either in whole or in part, since its founding.[26]

Cases Challenging the Legality of Official Presidential Actions

In addition to reviewing legislation enacted by Congress, the courts also can review the legality of executive orders and other actions taken by the president in his official capacity. One prominent example of this type of review can be seen in *Youngstown,* which we discussed in chapter 2. More recent examples include the judicial rulings that put several of President Trump's early executive orders on hold.

Courts also will review other types of official actions taken by the president. For example, consider the Supreme Court's review of President Franklin D. Roosevelt's decision to fire William Humphrey, a commissioner on the Federal Trade Commission. In 1931, President Hoover nominated (and the Senate confirmed) Humphrey to serve a seven-year term on the FTC. Yet when President Roosevelt entered the White House in 1933, he asked Humphrey to resign from his post. "I do not feel that your mind and my mind go along together on either the policies or the administering of the Federal Trade Commission, and, frankly, I think it is best for the people of this country that I should have a full confidence," Roosevelt explained to Humphrey.[27]

When Humphrey refused to resign, President Roosevelt fired him. Humphrey died soon after, but the representative of his estate pressed forward with a lawsuit against the United States challenging the legality of his termination. Humphrey's representative pointed to the congressional statute that had created the FTC. This statute specifies that the president may remove FTC commissioners only for certain discrete reasons, and not for the reasons Roosevelt gave.[28] In response, the president argued that the Constitution granted him the authority—regardless of what Congress enacted through statute—to fire officers, like Humphrey, who work within the executive branch.

In the end, the Supreme Court sided with Humphrey's representative. It ruled that Congress did have the power to place statutory limits on the president's ability to remove FTC commissioners such as Humphrey. As a result, Humphrey's representative was entitled to seek back pay from the United States (though not from President Roosevelt himself, as discussed below). The court's decision recognized a significant check on the president's power: namely, that Congress has at least some ability to restrict the president's removal powers.[29]

Another example of the judiciary's willingness to push back against the president came in *United States v. Nixon*,[30] a case decided in the midst of the Watergate scandal. It involved President Nixon's refusal to hand over tapes and documents relating to his conversations with aides. The dispute began when a district court judge, who had been presiding over a criminal case, ordered the president to hand over the materials in question. Nixon refused to do so. Instead, he took his case all the way to the Supreme Court. There, in a unanimous opinion, the Supreme Court ruled that Nixon had to turn over the tapes.

Nixon reacted by sequestering himself in the White House. No one knew whether he would obey the Supreme Court's order. As one scholar put it, the entire country "held its breath" to see whether the president would release the tapes.[31] In the meantime, an impeachment inquiry proceeded in the U.S. House of Representatives. When Nixon ultimately complied with the judiciary's ruling, the tapes suggested that Nixon himself had obstructed justice. This led to Nixon's downfall, prompting him to become the first U.S. president to resign from office—thereby confirming (at least indirectly) the vital role the courts play in checking the power of the presidency.

In short, the federal courts have been willing to review and even invalidate official presidential actions in many important contexts. In other contexts, however, they have taken a much more deferential approach. The courts have, for example, categorically refused to allow individuals to bring a particular type of lawsuit against a president. This impermissible type of lawsuit is one brought for money damages against the president himself (rather than against the United States more broadly, or against a president's subordinates), where the claim stems from any action the president has taken as part of his official duties. If a president were to illegally fire an employee of the executive branch, for example, and that employee were to seek damages against the president *himself*, rather than the United States or some other executive branch official, that lawsuit would go nowhere. Rather, the Supreme Court has decided that "in view of the special nature of the President's constitutional office and functions," the lawsuit cannot proceed.[32] A court would simply dismiss the claim.

The complicated balance the courts have struck in this area—allowing some lawsuits to go forward and dismissing others—reflects its effort to accommodate a host of difficult and often conflicting concerns. Among the most important are, on the one hand, giving the president the breathing room necessary for him to do his job effectively and, on the other, ensuring that the courts can do theirs. By insisting on policing this line, rather than simply acquiescing to the president, the courts protect their status as a powerful branch of government and serve as an important check on executive overreach.

Cases Challenging the Legality of Agency Action

The examples we have discussed so far involve the legality of a president's own actions. Yet a significant category of cases affecting presidential agendas involve challenges to the legality of actions taken by executive branch *agencies*, as well as by people working within those agencies. When the courts review these sorts of challenges, they tend to defer to agencies. In the words of Supreme Court Justice John Paul Stevens, this deference reflects our overall constitutional structure. It recognizes that judges are "not part of either political branch of the Government."[33] By contrast, an agency is governed by congressional statutes and housed within the executive branch. As such,

> an agency to which Congress has delegated policy-making responsibilities may . . . properly rely upon the incumbent administration's views of wise policy to inform its judgments. While agencies are not directly accountable to the people, the Chief Executive is, and it is entirely appropriate for

this political branch of the Government to make such policy choices—resolving the competing interests which Congress itself either inadvertently did not resolve, or intentionally left to be resolved by the agency charged with the administration of the statute in light of everyday realities.[34]

In short, according to Justice Stevens, "the responsibilities for assessing the wisdom of such policy choices and resolving the struggle between competing views of the public interest are not judicial ones."[35] Rather, "our Constitution vests such responsibilities in the political branches."[36]

Despite this deference, the courts still are willing to strike down agency action that crosses legal lines. One recent example helps to illustrate. When Obama first ran for office in 2008, he promised to raise the federal minimum wage. Once he was in office, he leaned hard on Congress in an effort to prod it to pass legislation that would accomplish this goal. When Congress failed to take action, Obama turned away from the legislative branch, and toward the executive branch. More specifically, he turned toward the Department of Labor (DOL).

Decades earlier, Congress had enacted a statute giving DOL the power to define certain exemptions from overtime pay standards. Committed to raising wages one way or another, Obama told DOL that it needed to use that decades-old power to revise the rules that govern overtime pay. After undergoing a lengthy rulemaking process, DOL issued new overtime standards that aimed to make millions more Americans eligible for mandatory overtime pay.[37] However, just days before the rule was to go into effect, a federal judge put it on hold. The judge reasoned, at least at the preliminary stages of the case, that DOL's overtime rule ran contrary to the statute that DOL's rule interpreted, and thus that it was legally impermissible.[38] When Obama left office in January 2017, the rule was still on hold.

After President Trump took office, his administration faced similar legal challenges. In particular, his administration's efforts to alter regulations—and often to rescind them—triggered an avalanche of legal challenges. While the law does allow agencies to rescind or to amend old regulations (even when a change in presidential administration provides the impetus), there are limits to how far they can go. On the one hand, "a change in administration brought about by the people casting their votes is a perfectly reasonable basis for an executive agency's reappraisal of the costs and benefits of its programs and regulations," in the words of Supreme Court Justice William Rehnquist.[39] On the other hand, even when an agency changes its mind, it still must remain "within the bounds established by Congress."[40] Among other things, the agency must be able to justify its reversal in light of relevant factors set forth in the statute, not by simply pointing to shifting political winds. These requirements have helped to motivate those opposing Trump's deregulatory agenda to file legal challenges. Indeed, in just the first year of Trump's presidency, many of the Trump Administration's attempts at rolling back regulations ran into complications in the federal courts.[41]

Cases Implicating Actions Taken by the President in His Personal Capacity

The three categories of cases we have just discussed—judicial review of legislation, judicial review of a president's official actions, and judicial review of agency actions—all involve actions taken by the government itself or by government officials working in their official capacities. None of these categories of cases involves actions that a president takes in his own *personal* capacity. Yet the federal courts also will, at times, review the legality of those actions, at least if they involve conduct that occurred before the president took office.

Cases involving the personal conduct of a sitting president are rare. The leading example is a case called *Clinton v. Jones.*[42] In that case, a former state employee named Paula Jones alleged that President Clinton had sexually harassed her when he was the governor of Arkansas. In response, Clinton argued that his status as president shielded him from the lawsuit, at least until he was no longer president. According to Clinton, being the President of the United States is such an all-consuming job that he needed to "devote his undivided time and attention to his public duties."[43] The Supreme Court disagreed. It ruled that Jones's case could move forward.

In reaching this conclusion, the court concluded that it was "highly unlikely" that the case would use up much of the president's time.[44] In addition, the court dismissed the idea that its ruling would somehow lead to a deluge of lawsuits that would "engulf the Presidency."[45] One justice, however, was not so sure about these predictions. Justice Stephen Breyer expressed concern that Jones's suit might well prove distracting to the president. As it turned out, Justice Breyer's fears were well founded: Jones's lawsuit fueled the Monica Lewinsky scandal, which in turn led the U.S. House of Representatives to impeach Clinton on charges of perjury and obstruction of justice. The entire affair almost toppled Clinton's presidency.

Nearly twenty years later, during President Trump's first year in office, the courts began grappling with issues similar to some of those presented in the *Clinton v. Jones* case. Given both the volume and the range of the lawsuits filed against President Trump, the federal courts again found themselves faced with the opportunity—and obligation—to begin to clarify how, when, and by whom a president can be sued.[46]

Courts and the Threat of a Constitutional Crisis

As we have discussed, the federal judiciary has served as a coequal branch of government throughout American history, with courts serving as a check on overreach by the other branches. Remarkably, the courts have accomplished this feat without their own enforcement mechanism. The federal courts have no army. They have no means by which to compel anyone—much less the president—to comply with their decisions. Instead, when the courts need help enforcing their rulings, they normally must turn to the executive branch, which does have enforcement powers. This dynamic helps to explain what happened during a famous confrontation in 1957 in Little Rock, Arkansas. White segregationists had tried to defy a court order to integrate a public school. In response, the federal courts had little recourse: They had no legal authority to send in troops to Little Rock or otherwise force compliance. Rather, the president at the time, President Dwight D. Eisenhower, was the one who ultimately had to decide whether it was appropriate to intervene. He decided it was and, through an executive order, instructed federal troops to escort the excluded students into the classroom.

The judicial branch's need to rely on the executive branch raises a disquieting question: What happens if the executive branch itself refuses to comply with a court ruling? What happens if the president himself is the subject of a direct order from a court—which he then openly defies?

Other than offering impeachment (or perhaps the Twenty-Fifth Amendment) as a possible solution to such a scenario, the law has no answer for what would happen. This is because such a situation would produce what many refer to as a constitutional crisis. While this term does not have a single, set definition, one way to think of it is as follows. A constitutional crisis is a serious problem that demands resolution but that constitutional principles do not resolve. Stated otherwise, the Constitution—and by extension, the statutes, regulations, and other laws that flow from the Constitution's basic structure—does not provide a way out. In a country governed by the rule of law, a constitutional crisis of this sort is concerning. It is also potentially destabilizing.

This helps to explain concerns that emerge when presidents aggressively criticize the courts, and in particular concerns that arose when President Trump very publicly expressed hostility toward the courts during his first year in office. While prior presidents had criticized court rulings, these earlier comments generally made clear each president's intention to comply with the rulings and otherwise confirmed a commitment to the rule of law. An illustrative comment came from President George W. Bush, who in 2008 voiced his displeasure with a Supreme Court decision rebuking his administration's stance on the rights of detainees in Guantánamo Bay.

"It was a deeply divided court," he said, "and I strongly agree with those who dissented." Bush nevertheless made sure to clarify what he meant: "We'll abide by the court's decision—that doesn't mean I have to agree with it."[47]

President Obama made a similarly critical comment at his 2010 State of the Union Address. Speaking about the Supreme Court's recent opinion in *Citizens United v. Federal Election Commission*, Obama pointedly asserted: "Last week, the Supreme Court reversed a century of law to open the floodgates for special interests—including foreign corporations—to spend without limit in our elections."[48]

These criticisms were biting. Yet they did not call into question the willingness of the presidents who made the statements to abide by the courts' decisions. Nor did they challenge the legitimacy of individual judges, or of the judiciary more generally.

President Trump's comments in his first year in office were of a different variety. When Judge Robart in Seattle halted Trump's first travel ban, for example, Trump directed his ire at the judge himself: "Just cannot believe a judge would put our country in such peril," Trump tweeted. "If something happens blame him and court system. People pouring in. Bad!"[49] The president further attempted to undermine Judge Robart by pointedly referring to him as a "so-called judge."[50] When a different federal judge—this one sitting in San Francisco—temporarily froze another executive order, the White House quickly denounced the ruling in a written statement that again questioned the legitimacy of the judiciary, calling the ruling an "egregious overreach by a single, unelected district judge."[51]

Not surprisingly, additional members of the judicial branch, along with many others, expressed concern about President Trump's comments. In particular, one federal judge—Judge Jay Bybee, an appointee of George W. Bush—went out of his way to comment on the impropriety of the attacks on the federal judiciary.

"The personal attacks on the distinguished district judge and our [judicial branch] colleagues were out of all bounds of civic and persuasive discourse," Judge Bybee wrote. "Such personal attacks treat the court as though it were merely a political forum in which bargaining, compromise, and even intimidation are acceptable principles. The courts of law must be more than that, or we are not governed by law at all."[52]

In making these remarks, Judge Bybee made clear that, in the case before him, he was actually sympathetic to President Trump's *legal* arguments. Judge Bybee, however, did not care for the *nonlegal* attacks on the judiciary.

Despite Trump's rhetoric, the president ultimately seemed to accept, in his first year of office, that the federal judiciary would be the one to determine the legality of at least some of his actions. Repeated assertions—all along the lines of his February 2017 all-caps tweet, "SEE YOU IN COURT"[53]—suggested that he was prepared to abide by the judiciary's orders.

In Sum: The Courts Often Insist on Having the Final Say

The federal judiciary operates as a significant check on the president. This is because the Constitution gives the courts the power, in limited but important circumstances, to provide relief to those who have been harmed by a president's refusal to follow the law. This all assumes, of course, that the president is willing to accept the courts' rulings as final and binding—an assumption that, as of 2017, has held true almost without exception throughout our country's history.

Still, bringing a lawsuit is costly, and it can be beyond the means of most individuals. Moreover, the rules governing how and when the courts will resolve these cases—including those relating to standing and the political question doctrine, as well as how and whether to sue the president himself—are complicated and require legal expertise to carefully parse. As a result, individuals seeking to harness the power of the courts to check a president (or, by contrast, seeking to help a president overcome checks coming from other quarters) might look to interest groups or other organizations that litigate on behalf of their members. As we discuss in chapter 8, these organizations frequently employ lawyers for precisely this purpose. Through such an approach, many have found success in their efforts to stop (or support) a president who has been skirting the legal line.

This all said, those interested in presidential politics should not limit their focus to the federal government. This is because our country also is governed by a system of state governments. As our next chapter will explain, the balance of power between the state and federal governments is a critical part of maintaining our democracy.

CHAPTER 7

How States Check the President

A healthy balance of power between the States and the Federal Government will reduce the risk of tyranny and abuse from either front.

— Justice Sandra Day O'Connor writing in 1991 for the U.S. Supreme Court in *Gregory v. Ashcroft*[1]

Who votes in U.S. elections? It depends on who is running. If a ballot includes a presidential race, more than half of eligible voters likely will vote. But if a ballot does not include a presidential candidate, turnout is likely to drop. By a *lot*. There is an irony to this discrepancy. Elected officials, including those elected to positions in state and local governments, exercise significant influence over a president's agenda. So if a voter cares about the presidential election, that voter should also care about state and local elections.

The U.S. Constitution gives state and local governments the power to support—or to push back against—a president's agenda. States have this freedom and flexibility because the Constitution does not allow a president to control state governments. Rather, as member states within a federation, states enjoy autonomy from the federal government. In this context, being a federation means that a government has two overlapping systems of government, with neither of the governments in charge of the other. California is not in charge of the United States, for example, and the United States is not in charge of California. Instead, both governments exist separately as sovereigns. As such, both have ways to resist the other.

Using immigration policy as a case study, this chapter explores the push and pull embedded in our federation. This analysis will show how state and local governments can affect federal policy—and, by extension, the president's ability to get things done. We begin with an overview of how our federal system works.

Splitting the "Atom of Sovereignty": The Nature of a Federation[2]

Each state within the union designs its own government in the manner it sees fit.[3] As it turns out, each state has decided to rely on the same three branches of government as has the federal government: executive, legislative, and judicial. These state branches are not identical to their federal counterparts, but they are similar. As a result, all state governments can pass, interpret, and enforce state laws. Each state also sits atop of (and exercises control over) a network of local governments, such as cities and counties.

As an example of how this overlapping system of governments works, take the authors of this book. We live near the campus of the University of Washington in Seattle, Washington. As a result, at least four governmental bodies exercise control over us: the United States, Washington State, King County, and the City of Seattle. The latter two governments—county and city—are ultimately a part of the Washington State government. By contrast, the first two governments—federal and state—are two separate governments, each with legal power over the other. And both with some form of control over us.

The laws governing federalism—that is, the laws governing the relationship between the federal and state governments—are vast and complicated. Yet three overarching principles (which we touched on in chapter 1) go far in explaining how this relationship works. First, whenever there is a conflict between a valid federal law and a state law, the federal law necessarily prevails.[4] The conflicting state law can no longer be enforced. (Recall our discussion of the conflict between federal and state law regarding the color of drug-packaging labels; those labels are going to be whatever color the federal law requires.) Federalism's second overarching principle recognizes that, despite this hierarchy, state governments often are the dominant players in enacting law. As such, state governments often are dominant in setting public policy. This is particularly true in areas where the federal government has not regulated, perhaps because the federal government does not have the legal power to do so.[5] Alternatively, the federal government might lack the political will to intervene in that area, or perhaps it simply has concluded that the issues are best addressed at the state level.

A prominent illustration of this second principle comes in the area of crime prevention and law enforcement. Imagine that someone is being investigated for committing a crime. In all likelihood, that person is being investigated for a state law crime, not for a federal law crime. Most of the criminal laws in our country are state laws. Now imagine that a person gets arrested. In all likelihood, this person has been arrested by an officer employed by a state or local government, not by the federal government. Now imagine an individual is being hauled into court for committing a crime. In all likelihood, that prosecution will occur in a state court, not a federal court. Finally, imagine someone incarcerated for committing a crime. That person in all likelihood will be imprisoned in a state-affiliated prison, not in a federally affiliated prison. Indeed, in recent years, well over 80 percent of those incarcerated are in state-affiliated prisons.[6] In short, when it comes to criminal law proceedings in the United States, the vast majority of work is done by the states, with little to no involvement by federal authorities.

Still, the federal government does investigate and prosecute some crimes, such as those associated with federal tax evasion and violations of the federal drug laws. Even here, though, federal authorities often need the assistance of their state counterparts to get the job done. Federal officials (such as FBI agents) may feel it is helpful, and perhaps even necessary, to work closely with local detectives on a case relating to, say, a multistate methamphetamine drug ring. These local detectives are neither employed nor controlled by the federal government. Yet without their help, the FBI agents may find themselves logistically unable to get the information they need to properly pursue their own federal cases. So even when the federal government is itself enforcing the criminal laws, it often leans heavily on state authorities.

In this way, criminal law provides a striking illustration of the balance of power between the state and federal governments. A similar dynamic emerges elsewhere. States tend to be the dominant government when it comes to property rights, contractual rights, family-related legal issues, and many other areas of the law that affect people on a daily basis. Even in areas where the federal government tends to exercise more control than the state governments (such as in the area of immigration), the federal government still relies heavily on the assistance of state authorities.

Indeed, when it comes to this particular area—immigration—the relationship between the state and federal governments is so involved, and so important, that it provides a helpful lens through which to analyze what exactly the law allows states to do. This brings us to federalism's third overarching principle, which goes to the autonomy that states enjoy. Because states are their own sovereign governments, the law generally allows them to *choose* whether to enforce or otherwise carry out the federal government's policies.[7] This autonomy does not mean that states can flout generally applicable federal laws that regulate states in the same way that the laws regulate private parties. For example, states cannot refuse to pay their employees in accordance with federal minimum wage laws that regulate employers, public and private, across the country.[8] Rather, this autonomy means that the states generally need not assist the federal government in developing federal regulatory schemes or executing federal laws. For example, states cannot be forced to conduct background checks for the federal government.[9] And states cannot be forced to arrest people on behalf of the federal government.[10] Rather, each state is legally allowed to choose whether to support, or to push back against, the national government's policies, including those of the president.

If a state wishes to support a president, it has many options. It can, for example, offer the services of state employees to help the president with his preferred projects. Alternatively, states can work to obstruct the president's agenda. A state can refuse to offer the help of its employees, for example, even if the president asks for assistance or offers to pay for it. As the following discussion reveals, states have taken these steps—and many more—in the context of the complex constellation of policies that shape federal immigration law.

Immigration as an Illustration:
States Working in *Support* of the Federal Government

When we refer to immigration policy, we are referring to the collection of rules directed at people who would like to enter or live within the United

States but who are not American citizens. Different people have different views on what constitutes the best immigration policies—and that range of disagreement certainly holds true at the presidential level. Yet one thing that nearly everyone agrees on is that, as a practical matter, the federal government cannot do this work all by itself. Rather, to effectively execute the nation's immigration laws (a task that ultimately falls on the president, as head of the executive branch), the federal government needs the help of state and local governments.

Prior to his inauguration, President Trump indicated that he planned to oversee the deportation of two to three million unauthorized immigrants. Yet no president can accomplish such a massive undertaking simply by issuing orders. The deportation of each individual person requires a great deal of work, by many different people. Each deportation requires, among other things, that officials identify the individual in question, prove that deportation is legally authorized, allow that individual to respond and contest that conclusion, detain that person as considered necessary, and, finally, physically remove that individual from the country.[11] Each step requires the work of public officials, whether they are agents of Immigration and Customs Enforcement, judges, government lawyers, or others. Multiply the work that goes into deporting one person by several million, and you begin to see one of the biggest challenges facing President Trump's promises of widespread immigration crackdowns: not only securing the funding from Congress needed to pay for all this activity, but also finding even close to enough officials to do the work. To put this challenge into perspective, one judge writing in 2015 noted that "although there are approximately 11.3 million removable aliens in this country today, for the last several years Congress has provided the Department of Homeland Security (DHS) with only enough resources to remove approximately 400,000 [annually]."[12]

These sorts of resource limitations help to explain why the federal government tries to rely on state and local governments—and especially on state and local law-enforcement officers—for assistance. For a state or a local government that wants to support the federal government's immigration policies, there are many things it can do to help. A state, for example, can encourage its law-enforcement officers to turn over information they have gathered, including information about potentially deportable individuals, to the federal government. Likewise, employees of city jails can give federal agents notice if they are planning to release a noncitizen from detention. Through actions like these, a state or local government helps to advance federal investigations and relieve federal agents of some of their workload.

A state or local government also can help advance federal policies by enacting laws in support of the federal government's efforts. In 2010, for example, Arizona enacted a statute that, among other things, required its officers to verify a person's immigration status with the federal government when making certain stops, detentions, or arrests. Asked to review the legality of this Arizona statute, the U.S. Supreme Court confirmed that states may enact laws of this sort so long as they do not violate the Constitution's protections of individual rights or otherwise conflict with federal law.[13] (Other requirements contained in this Arizona statute did conflict with federal law, according to the Supreme Court, and so it stopped Arizona from enforcing them.)

Yet another way state and local governments can assist the federal government is by filing supportive arguments in court. In the immigration context, states have filed numerous legal briefs—called amicus briefs—to try to convince the courts that the federal government's position is correct and that the states' perspectives are particularly valuable in understanding the legal challenge and its implications.

State and local actions like these make a big difference to the federal government's ability to enforce the immigration laws. In the words of one scholar, "for better and for worse, effective federal immigration enforcement often depends upon the extensive participation of state and local officials."[14] As a result, decisions by state and local officials, including decisions regarding whether and how to provide assistance to the federal government, can significantly affect a president's immigration-related efforts.

Immigration as an Illustration:
States Working to *Resist* the Federal Government

Just as states can work to support the president's agenda, they can work against it. One forceful way for state and local governments to oppose the president is to drag him and his subordinates into court. This sort of litigation can cover a range of issues—from health care to the environment to labor disputes. Yet even if we limit ourselves only to the area of immigration, litigation abounds. To take a recent example, in March 2017, the City of San Francisco and Santa Clara County sued President Trump over his threats to punish so-called sanctuary cities. The term "sanctuary cities" (or "sanctuary jurisdictions") is not well defined, but it tends to refer to state or local governments that have declined, in one way or another, to help the federal government enforce the immigration laws. As of 2017, this list includes Oregon, New York City, and New Orleans, among many others. Given how much assistance the federal government needs to enforce its immigration laws, refusals of this sort by state or local jurisdictions can hamstring federal immigration policies, including aggressive plans for deportation.

Yet the Constitution, as interpreted by the federal courts, empowers state and local jurisdictions to resist the federal government in this way. More specifically, the Constitution prohibits the president (or anyone in the federal government) from "commandeering" the state or local governments.[15] By extension, it prohibits the federal government from commandeering state or local officials, including law-enforcement officers.[16] The president cannot hire these state and local officials, he cannot fire them, and he cannot force them to engage in official governmental activities. As a result, if the president wants to expand the number of undocumented people the federal government is deporting, he cannot force state officers to assist with detention and deportation.[17] What the federal government can do is try to entice the states to volunteer such assistance, such as by offering money in exchange.[18] In addition, the federal government can, of course, choose to allocate its own resources to reflect the priorities it feels are the most important. However, any effort to force the states to actively assist in deporting individuals would be unconstitutional.[19] State and local jurisdictions can use their constitutional protections to push back.

States seeking to resist federal immigration policies have yet another means of doing so. Namely, they can pass laws that fill gaps left open by the federal government. States like California, Nevada, and Washington, for example, have passed laws allowing unauthorized immigrants to obtain driver's licenses. It is true that this power—to enact laws in tension with federal law—is limited, given federalism's first principle: that state law falls whenever it conflicts with federal law.[20] Still, the states do have at least some room to maneuver in this space, and that flexibility is important.

In short, state or local governments have many options available when deciding how to respond to a president's agenda. This leads to questions concerning how exactly such a government decides which step to take. Who decides that some states, like Texas, will so often resist the policies of someone like President Obama and so often support those of someone like President Trump? And who decides that other states, like California, will so often do the opposite? The answer is: whoever is elected into state and local office. If voters elect members of the Republican Party into office at the state and local level, those state and local government representatives are more likely to support the policies of a Republican president—and vice versa.

In Sum: States Have Significant Autonomy

Given that the United States is a federation, rather than a unitary state, our national government often has to rely on the voluntary assistance of state and local governments to get things done. In light of this dynamic, state and local governments have a special ability to help or to hinder a president's agenda. Those who care about a president's agenda therefore should also care about the agendas of those elected to state and local office. Constituents might consider involving themselves in state and local governments, including reaching out to let their representatives know how they would like them to proceed. Eligible voters should endeavor to vote in all elections, including those for state and local positions—and might even consider running for office themselves.

Still, those working inside the government, whether state or federal, are not the only ones affecting the president's agenda. As our next chapter explains, people working outside the government also exercise influence over, and often serve as an important check on, the federal government.

CHAPTER 8

How Outsiders Check the President

All free governments are managed by the combined wisdom and folly of the people.

— James A. Garfield writing as a member of the House of Representatives in 1880, a year before he would take office as president[1]

Of all the people the law empowers to check a president, many do not work for the government. This outside pressure comes from disparate sources. Three of the most important are the media, interest groups, and voters. All are protected to some degree by the law. Collectively, these forces serve as a powerful check on anyone serving in an official government position, including the president. This chapter explores each of these three important categories of nongovernmental actors.

Outside the Government: How the Press Checks the President

The relationship between the media and the presidency is complicated, to put it mildly. Take Thomas Jefferson. Prior to becoming president, he paid homage to the press, proclaiming boldly that "were it left to me to decide whether we should have a government without newspapers, or newspapers without a government, I should not hesitate a moment to prefer the latter."[2] Indeed, he took full advantage of the press to circulate vitriol about his political rival, John Adams. Yet by the end of his second term in office—after the media exposed a relationship he had with a young enslaved woman—Jefferson's views had dimmed.

"Nothing can now be believed which is seen in a newspaper,"

Jefferson wrote, disdain saturating the page. "Truth itself becomes suspicious by being put into that polluted vehicle."[3]

"Polluted" or not, the work of the media profoundly affects a president's ability to move his agenda forward. Sometimes it helps a media-savvy president. President Theodore Roosevelt, for example, frequently invited journalists to the White House to share his thoughts. He found this opportunity to persuade so valuable that he coined the term "bully pulpit" to describe its power.

Other times, the press acts as a significant check on the president and the executive branch more generally. One example of this power revealed itself in dramatic fashion in the summer of 2013. Scared and secretive, multiple doctors urgently contacted CNN. These doctors—employed by the federal government's Department of Veterans Affairs (VA), an agency within the executive branch that falls under the president's supervision—had responded with alarm to the negligence and malfeasance they had seen from the inside. When efforts at internal reform failed, the doctors turned to the media. After months of research, CNN broke the story.[4] Long waits for care at VA hospitals had caused the deaths of numerous military veterans. Yet rather than work to remedy the problems, senior staff members had covered up delays, employees had altered and destroyed records, and threats of reprisal had intimidated people into silence.

CNN's allegations were explosive, and the outrage lit a fire. In response, the government finally moved into action, with Congress, the White House, and the VA itself all launching their own investigations. Each confirmed the same thing: that deep dysfunction was indeed plaguing the department. Within months of CNN's first incendiary report, the head of the VA—an official hand-selected by the president and confirmed by the Senate—accepted responsibility and resigned. The Department of Justice opened a criminal investigation. Congress passed, and President Obama signed into law, the Veterans' Access to Care through Choice, Accountability, and Transparency Act, which sought to reform the VA and provide additional funding. Though government reform often proceeds at a glacial pace, it moved like lightning in response to the VA scandal. The media had played a pivotal role in influencing the workings of the executive branch—and, more generally, our system of checks and balances.

CNN's exposé of dysfunction at the VA provides just one illustration of the media's power to check the government. There are many more. One of the most consequential arose out of Watergate in the 1970s, when articles published by outlets like the *Washington Post, Time,* and the *New York Times* began to uncover increasingly damning reports of what appeared to be criminal activity going all the way to the very top of the executive branch. This journalism helped to provide Congress and the courts with what they needed to battle a relentlessly recalcitrant president. This combination of investigative journalism coupled with checks wielded by the legislative and judicial branches eventually led to President Nixon's resignation.

To an important degree, this complicated relationship between the press and the presidency is maintained by legal principles and protections. Among the most prominent are those emanating from the First Amendment of the Constitution.[5] Over time, courts have interpreted the First Amendment to forbid government actors in all three branches of government, at both the federal and state levels, from abridging freedom of speech and the press. The courts have further interpreted these prohibitions as protecting a broad range of actors—not only institutional media outlets like the *Wall Street Journal* and Fox News but any person or organization wishing to communicate something publicly in writing or orally.[6] This broad scope of First Amendment protections is particularly important given that more than half of the adults in the United States now get at least some of their news through social media platforms like Facebook and Twitter.[7]

The very strong protections the First Amendment grants to speakers help to explain why Arthur Sulzberger, the publisher of the *New York Times,* felt emboldened in 1971 to commit the journalistic equivalent of swinging a bat at a beehive. While Nixon was president, Sulzberger approved the publication of the Pentagon Papers, a top-secret Department of Defense study leaked by an insider. (The individual who leaked the study was one of the whistleblowers we discussed in chapter 5.) This study confirmed that in the Vietnam War's buildup and execution, the United States had repeatedly misled its people about the scope of the government's involvement in the region. Its publication threatened to, and eventually did, trigger widespread outrage.

In response, Nixon's administration pressured the *New York Times* to stop publishing the study, which it had been planning to release in excerpts, one day at a time. When that pressure failed, the administration hauled the newspaper into court to force it to halt publication. The case quickly worked its way up to the Supreme Court, which ruled decisively in the newspaper's favor.

The court began by emphasizing the vigor with which the First Amendment resists governmental censorship, particularly when the government seeks to censor prior to publication.[8] The court then quickly concluded that the Nixon Administration's justifications (primarily relating to national security) were not enough to overcome this legal barrier. One justice homed in on the significant role that the First Amendment plays in the power struggle between the president and the press. "The executive branch seems to have forgotten the essential purpose and history of the First Amendment," Justice Hugo Black wrote, as he explained that the amendment was meant to protect individual liberty as well as to "curtail and restrict the general powers granted to the Executive, Legislative, and Judicial Branches."[9] And indeed the First Amendment did, in this case, restrict the president's powers. Not only did it thwart the Nixon Administration's efforts to stymie the *New York Times*; it also allowed the American people access to information that was critical of the United States government.

Still, the law of the First Amendment is complicated and nuanced. Rather than interpret the First Amendment in a one-size-fits-all manner that prohibits the government from placing any and all restrictions on speech or the press, the courts have interpreted the Constitution to provide protections only in some circumstances. For example, the First Amendment has been interpreted to protect the publication of some statements, even false ones, made about the conduct of public officials. Yet these same protections will not hold if statements are made with knowledge of their falsity or with reckless disregard of their falsity. The court decisions setting forth this careful balance, including a landmark case called *New York Times Co. v. Sullivan*,[10] help to put into context the threats that governmental actors occasionally make against the press.

On the campaign trail, for example, Trump promised to "open

up our libel laws so when [media outlets] write purposely negative and horrible and false articles, we can sue them and win lots of money."[11] He continued, naming specific targets. "So when the *New York Times* writes a hit piece which is a total disgrace or when the *Washington Post* . . . writes a hit piece, we can sue them and win money instead of having no chance of winning because they're totally protected."[12] Despite this bluster, if any government official—even the president—were to try to sue a news outlet in response to negative press coverage (or, for that matter, to change the laws in an attempt to facilitate such lawsuits), the First Amendment would pose a significant legal barrier.

This is not to suggest that the First Amendment protects against all possible repercussions for government-related speech. Particularly when national security is involved, the Constitution's protections may eventually give way. This helps to explain why, in unusual circumstances, individuals may be punished for the unauthorized disclosure of information about the government. Chelsea Manning serves as an example. Manning was a U.S. Army intelligence analyst when, in the course of her employment, she obtained access to information concerning the Iraq and Afghanistan wars. In 2010, she made this information public through the WikiLeaks organization, which worked with traditional news outlets, such as the *New York Times*, to disseminate the information. The Obama Administration responded by bringing criminal charges against Manning. In 2013, she was convicted and sentenced to several decades' worth of prison time.[13]

Whether the federal government might be able, in future cases, to take the next step—that is, to prosecute not only leakers such as Manning, but also the organizations and reporters helping to disseminate the leaked information—is a matter of legal debate. The law that would govern such prosecutions remains hazy,[14] in part because the federal government historically has not made a practice of prosecuting members of the media who publicize leaked information. Yet past restraint is no promise of future restraint, and at some point the federal government very well may try to bring criminal charges against members of the media.

Prosecutions like Manning's, combined with other forms of pressure that in recent years have been placed on leakers and journalists, have caused concern and frustration among many members of the press.

Accusing the Obama Administration of proving to be unexpectedly hostile toward the media, these journalists have expressed fear that President Trump's administration will likewise push the legal limits in cracking down on independent journalism. In response to such developments, the First Amendment will continue to provide an imperfect, but still powerful, backstop.

Another important source of legal power for the press is contained in a federal statute called the Freedom of Information Act.[15] This law allows any "person"—including any individual, association, or organization—to file requests to view records created by the executive branch of the United States government. While the law (often referred to as FOIA) is subject to a complicated assortment of exceptions and conditions, its main thrust is straightforward: It provides a check on the executive branch by forcing it to turn over information about what it is doing.

Reporters for the *Oregonian* newspaper, for example, relied in part on FOIA requests to dig deeper into an investigative study of the U.S. Immigration and Naturalization Service (INS), which was part of the Department of Justice during the Clinton Administration. The reporters had been uncovering stories of the INS mistreating people and abusing its powers. In 1999, the INS held one teenager from China in jail for weeks even after she had obtained asylum. In another case, it deported a mother from Germany for an expired visa after jailing her, strip-searching her, and forcing her to leave the country without her breastfeeding daughter. To provide additional context for these sorts of cruelties, one journalist sent FOIA requests to district offices across the country, requesting records concerning the criteria that each office had used to evaluate the performance of its officers. The series that emerged from these investigations, titled "Liberty's Heavy Hand," won the 2001 Pulitzer Prize for public service, in part because of the reforms it had prompted.

Another way to confirm FOIA's importance is to recognize how aggressively the executive branch resists its reach. In 1974, President Ford went so far as to veto an expansion of the law even though it enjoyed widespread, bipartisan support—such sweeping support, in fact, that Congress overrode the president's veto. Decades later, President Obama triggered criticism when news agencies learned that his administration had spent a record $36.2 million in a single year on legal fees defending its various refusals to release FOIA-requested information. During that same year (2016), the Obama Administration received nearly 800,000 FOIA requests, spent nearly $500 million answering those requests, and employed more than 4,000 full-time FOIA employees.[16]

In 2017, President Trump quickly found his administration subject to a similar onslaught. Indeed, one Trump-related FOIA request hit officials even before he took office. On January 19, 2017, one day before Trump's inauguration, the ACLU submitted a request "for records pertaining to financial and other ethical conflicts of interest in connection with the presidential transition of [the] President-Elect."[17]

As these illustrations confirm, a long-standing power struggle characterizes the media, the president, and laws that govern their complicated exchanges. Recently, President Trump's exceptionally brazen attacks on the media have further complicated—and deepened—this struggle. In addition to threatening the press with litigation, Trump has publicly and repeatedly derided mainstream press outlets as "very, very dishonest," as "disgusting and corrupt," and as "fake news," among other epithets.[18] On February 17, 2017, the president went still further, invoking a phrase that, by virtue of its use in autocratic regimes deeply hostile to the press, has taken on ominous overtones. "The FAKE NEWS media (failing @nytimes, @NBCNews, @ABC, @CBS, @CNN) is not my enemy," Trump tweeted. "It is the enemy of the American People!"[19]

Developments like these concern many who study democratic governments. Although media outlets do enjoy legal protections, an executive branch hostile to a free press can exert strong forms of pressure to resist the media's speech: through intrusive investigations of journalists, burdensome lawsuits (which impose costs even if a journalist ultimately prevails), and aggressive actions that come right up to, and perhaps even cross, legal lines.

To some, this sort of threat is particularly concerning given competing pressures the contemporary media also face. Such pressures include the increasing political polarization of the media, with some in the country turning exclusively to right-leaning news outlets while others resort to their left-leaning counterparts. In addition, the media must grapple with the difficulties posed by what is emerging as a true "fake news" industry—as illustrated, for example, by activities in the country of Macedonia, where local teenagers developed and circulated verifiably false "news" stories during the 2016 election. These teenagers made thousands of dollars by plagiarizing false stories from disreputable websites and repackaging them for Facebook—where they were then viewed and shared widely.[20] These sorts of activities add yet another layer to the challenges already facing the media in the internet age. Among the most important of those is the need to make money to sustain what has always been an extremely resource-intensive process of uncovering stories, fact-checking content, and turning it all into readable copy.

Whether more traditional media outlets can survive this onslaught—and whether the press more generally can maintain its independence as a critical and irreplaceable check on the president and other members of government—may depend on the press's ability to convince the public of the value it serves in our system. More specifically, it may depend on the degree to which various actors, including the public itself, are able to recognize the importance of the press and to do what it takes to support its independence, such as by paying for access to reputable and reliable journalism.

Outside the Government: How Interest Groups Check the President

A second source of outside influence emerges from what are known as "interest groups." Judging by the rhetoric used in campaigns, interest groups very well may be the least popular, but most powerful, players in politics. As a candidate for president, Hillary Clinton blamed interest groups for "doing too much to rig the game" and vowed to support an agenda opposed to their ends.[21] Trump, in turn, promised to eliminate their influence over government and accused Clinton of seeking to enrich her "special interest friends" by plotting "the destruction of U.S. sovereignty."[22]

Despite the negativity and bluster surrounding interest groups, these organizations are diverse in their goals and effects, and collectively they serve as a very powerful check on the government, including the president. As a result, it is important to understand the ways they affect United States politics—even if, ultimately, the law plays only a limited role in shaping their involvement.

The term "interest group" is vague, and the Constitution never mentions it. Defined generally, an interest group is simply an association of people or entities that is working on behalf of a particular cause. Any cause! So understood, the universe of interest groups is practically endless. It includes charitable associations, professional organizations, trade associations, civil rights organizations, and any number of additional groups. Among the most prominent interest groups are the AARP (formerly the American Association of Retired Persons), the American Civil Liberties Union (ACLU), the American Federation of Labor and Congress of Industrial Organizations (AFL-CIO), the American Israel Public Affairs Committee (AIPAC), the National Right to Life Committee (NRLC), the National Association for the Advancement of Colored People (NAACP), and the National Rifle Association (NRA). And this list, of course, just barely scratches the surface. Don't forget various Tea Party organizations, the various Indivisible organizations (a collection of groups arising out of the 2016 elections that purport to be liberal counterparts to the Tea Party), and the near-limitless list of groups that compete for their politically minded supporters.

What are all these groups for? Essentially, they seek to advance certain causes on behalf of their members. The range of causes they advance is as diverse as the groups themselves. These causes might include the protection of specific industries (solar energy, real estate, weapons manufacture, walnut growing, or anything else that generates revenue), the protection of underserved communities (the poor, the sick, or those who otherwise could use additional assistance), the expansion or reduction of environmental regulations, the imposition or rejection of gun control, the advancement of pro-life or pro-choice causes, and a whole litany of additional, often conflicting ends. Given this vast diversity in organizations and interests, it is difficult to generalize about interest groups in the United States. Still, at least one thing is clear: These associations are very influential in American politics.

As a legal matter, interest groups enjoy this powerful position in part due to the First Amendment, including the amendment's guarantees of freedom of speech, petition, and assembly. Partially as a result of these legal protections, interest groups can (and routinely do) engage in a range of politically directed activities. These activities include lobbying, involvement in agency rulemaking, litigation, and election-related participation. To varying degrees, the law protects the ability of interest groups to participate in each of these activities.[23]

Lobbying

Using the power of influence, lobbyists can directly affect the work of the federal government. Lobbyists working on behalf of the American Medical Association, for example, might meet with a member of Congress regarding a proposed health-care reform and pressure that representative to vote in a particular way. Effective lobbyists are able to exert significant influence in Washington, D.C.—so much so that one former representative, a thirty-four-year veteran of the House of Representatives, has referred to lobbyists as supplanting the media as the unofficial "fourth branch of government."[24]

The law governing lobbyists is complicated. Congress has attempted to regulate their activities through, for example, requirements that lobbyists regularly disclose information about their work and expenditures. However, these regulations still allow lobbyists wide latitude. Moreover, because the First Amendment arguably protects much of what lobbyists do, it would be difficult for the government to impose serious legal restrictions on lobbyists even if it were inclined to do so.[25]

Participating in Rulemaking

By participating in the rulemaking process, interest groups can influence the many regulations that are issued by executive branch agencies. As we discussed in chapter 3, the law often precludes an agency from making, amending, or rescinding a regulation unless it first undertakes a lengthy notice-and-comment rulemaking process. During this process, interested members of the public, including interest groups, can submit their thoughts about the proposed regulation. The agency is then required by law to consider and respond to all significant comments that it receives before making any final decisions. If the agency fails to adequately fulfill this task, its decision risks invalidation by a later legal challenge. Interest groups often get deeply involved in this notice-and-comment process, and their submissions can encourage agencies to go in different directions when issuing regulations.

Interest groups looking to influence rulemaking also might file what is called a petition for rulemaking. These petitions, which are some-times referred to as citizen petitions, allow an interest group (or any other entity or individual) to make the case that an agency should adopt or change a regulation. The law generally gives agencies wide latitude to reject these petitions for rulemaking. Still, the courts can push back against an agency's refusal to adequately respond to such a submission. As we will discuss in chapter 9, an extremely important Supreme Court decision on climate change involved a citizen petition, submitted by interest groups, that the EPA initially had denied.

Litigating

Interest groups also can attempt to advance their agenda through the courts. A group such as the ACLU, for example, spends a great deal of its time and resources bringing lawsuits against government actors. In 2017, the ACLU was among those suing the federal government in response to the travel bans imposed after President Trump assumed office. Yet the ACLU has been suing executive branch officials for decades. To take but one example, in 2013, it sued Obama-era federal officials in response to data-collection practices adopted by the National Security Agency. Join-ing the ACLU is a long list of interest groups similarly inclined to sue the president and his officials in response to perceived overreaching. For example, the U.S. Chamber of Commerce joined or initiated multiple lawsuits against members of President Obama's administration, while the Constitutional Accountability Center has done the same with lawsuits brought against President Trump and his administration.

Participating in Elections

Interest groups also can engage in activities meant to influence which candidates are elected into office. Interest groups participate in the elec-tions process through numerous means, including by running many of the ads you might be forced to sit through in the run-up to an election. A complicated set of legal rules imposes some restrictions on the ways that interest groups can participate in these political activities. However, due in part to the protections provided by the First Amendment, these restrictions are limited and not particularly effective.

This list of activities is far from exhaustive, as interest groups find many additional ways to advance their agendas. What all these activities have in common is that they reflect the power of concentrated interests. Able to pull together significant resources through organization and outreach, these groups direct their efforts toward narrow and targeted ends.

In American politics, this approach tends to work. As a result, an effective and well-supported interest group can be one of the most powerful checks on any governmental official, and certainly on the president.

Outside the Government: How Voters Check the President

Voting provides yet another powerful means of checking a president. But not just voting in presidential elections—voting in *all* elections.

It is true that voters hold a president directly accountable (by voting him either into or out of office) only once every four years. Moreover, because the Constitution allows a president to run for reelection only once, a president can serve out his second term without the threat of being rejected by the voters. Yet if we focus only on presidential elections, we overlook the profound importance of other elections and other offices. Given how much the president must rely on other governmental actors, voters who participate in every election are particularly powerful players.

Take the national midterm elections that occur in the years between presidential elections. In these midterms, one-third of the seats in the Senate are up for election, as are all the seats in the House of Representatives. Given just how much control Congress exercises over the executive branch, these elections have an enormous influence on what the president can accomplish. President Obama's experience helps to illustrate. Obama was able to advance his agenda significantly in his first two years in office, 2009 and 2010. He oversaw the passage of an enormous economic stimulus. He helped to design and implement sweeping reform of banks and other financial institutions. And he successfully pushed for the enactment of the Affordable Care Act.

In the following two years, by contrast, Obama found most of his efforts stymied. What explains the change? The midterm elections. For Obama's first two years in office, he had enjoyed a Congress controlled by members of his own party. While these various Democratic politicians did not agree on everything, they agreed on much, and that agreement was reflected in the progress the president made. Obama's ability to advance his agenda, however, suffered a dire blow when his party lost seats in the 2010 midterm elections. On that election night, in November 2010, the Democratic president saw a thoroughly blue Congress—packed with a majority of Democrats in the House and a near filibuster-proof supermajority in the Senate—swept away by a red wave of Republicans. As a result of those elections (and in particular the Democrats' loss of the House majority), the Obama Administration began to hit often-insurmountable roadblocks.

Obama's experience illustrates a more general truth: So-called "down-ballot races" can significantly affect a president's ability to advance his own agenda. A down-ballot race is an election that is not as well known as the most high-profile elections (and that is, more often than not, listed farther down on the actual ballot). Among the races frequently considered down ballot are those for state positions, including state legislators, state attorneys general, and governors, as well as for local positions, such as county executives, mayors, and city council members. Elections over U.S. congressional seats can fall into this category as well.

These down-ballot races often unfold in the shadow of more high-profile elections. Yet they are profoundly important. These races produce the representatives and officials who, for example, vote on whether to enact legislation that helps or hinders the president with respect to the budget (in the case of members of Congress); decide whether to fortify or dismantle sanctuary cities and other locally based resistance (in the case of local officials); and determine whether to sue the federal government for perceived overreaching in response to expansive new federal programs (in the case of state attorneys general).

State officials, including state legislators and secretaries of state, also are empowered to enact and enforce many of the rules that govern *future* elections—including future federal elections. (Although the federal government also plays an important role in setting and enforcing election-related rules, its involvement in this regard is generally much less significant than that of its state counterparts.) These state officials can decide, among other things, who can vote and under what circumstances, all within the more general boundaries set by federal statutory law, as well as by state and federal constitutional law. In many states, state legislators also are the ones who draw the geographical lines governing elections, through a process called redistricting (or, to its many critics, "gerrymandering"). The power to draw these lines—and more generally to set the rules of an election—is an enormously important power. This is because the outcome of any election depends, to a limited but significant degree, on the rules that govern how it is run.

To take one recent example of the importance of election-related laws, consider the 2016 presidential elections. If our national elections for president had been based purely on who received the largest share of the votes nationwide, then, all else being equal, Hillary Clinton would have been elected president in 2016, with approximately sixty-six million votes. Donald Trump would have been the runner-up, with approximately sixty-three million votes.[26] However, this is not how the rules of presidential elections work. Rather, the rules established by the Constitution provide that each state has a given number of electoral votes (based on a set formula), and the winner of the presidential election is the candidate who receives a majority of those state-based electoral votes. Under this latter set of rules—which, of course, was the set of rules that drove each candidate's campaign strategies in the 2016 elections—Trump was the clear victor, with 304 electoral votes out of a possible 538.[27]

Virtually every rule that governs an election has some effect, however subtle, on its likely outcome. Take, as another example, state-enacted voter ID laws. These laws require individuals to show identification before they can vote. To many supporters of these laws, a voter ID requirement seems like a sensible response to the perceived threat of voting-related fraud. To many opponents, however, these laws are objectionable due to the lack of supporting evidence for widespread voting fraud, questions over whether voter ID actually serves as a meaningful check on fraud, and concerns over how these laws can interfere with eligible voters' ability to cast a ballot. What has become common wisdom amid this debate is that these laws tend to affect certain groups disproportionately. More specifically, these laws tend to help Republican candidates and hurt Democratic candidates. This dynamic helps to explain, at least in part, why Republican politicians tend to be in favor of voter ID laws while Democratic politicians tend to oppose them.

Across the country, state election laws vary quite a bit. Still, the

Constitution, combined with federal statutes, does provide some baseline protections for all Americans regarding the right to vote. If a voter can prove that a state intentionally discriminated against voters of a given race, for example, then a court likely will force that state to change its practices. These protections are extremely important because, as noted, the laws governing elections have the potential to affect who gets elected.

Regardless of the specific rules governing elections, however, the fundamental point remains: Voting matters. By extension, voters matter. When it comes to presidential elections, many people understand just how important their votes are. However, by also participating in mid-term, down-ballot, and local elections, voters can make a much more significant difference, one that affects even the highest levels of government.

In Sum: Outsiders Can Influence Presidential Politics

Discussions of checks and balances often focus on governmental actors: on members of the three federal branches and on state and local officials. Yet the law also empowers those outside the government who in many respects serve as a counterforce to those in power. Members of the media, for example, wield legally protected tools that allow them to serve as a vital check on the president and other members of government. Interest groups also exercise significant political influence, as they engage in a wide range of activities for a wide range of purposes. Finally, voters have profound effects on politics by helping to determine who gets to exercise the power of the government (including the power to further check and balance) in the first place. These disparate forces affect the ability of any president to shape our country—and the world. To that end, the power of all these actors reveals itself vividly in our next chapter, which illustrates the limits of presidential power as it relates to a problem of truly global proportions: climate change.

CHAPTER 9

Climate Change: A Case Study

The question is not whether we need to act ... [T]he question now is whether we will have the courage to act before it's too late. And how we answer will have a profound impact on the world that we leave behind not just to you, but to your children and to your grandchildren.

— President Barack Obama speaking about climate change in 2013[1]

The law gives the president enormous power. Yet, as this book has demonstrated, the law also imposes real limits on that power. As a result, the advancement of a president's agenda often depends less on a president's own force of will than on the cooperation of other actors. To illustrate how this dynamic can play out in practice, we turn to the federal government's response to climate change.

Although this story begins decades ago with a congressional statute signed into law by President Nixon, more recently elected presidents, including Presidents Obama and Trump, serve in the starring roles. Pushed into this position by decades of legislative gridlock in response to climate change, these presidents have witnessed environmental groups, various states, and members of the public turn toward the executive branch to demand action. At the same time, fossil-fuel interests, different states, and other members of the public have tried to convince these presidents to take a hands-off approach to climate change.

In one presidential administration—Obama's—calls to combat climate change resulted in significant regulatory action. But precisely because these actions occurred through the executive branch, rather than the legislative branch, subsequent presidential administrations have the power to undo much of what Obama accomplished. Indeed, in President Trump's first few months in office, he began the process of dismantling many key Obama-era climate policies. This back-and-forth among the presidents helps to confirm both the scope and the limits of presidential power.

The work of others in the area of climate change further illustrates the boundaries of presidential power. While Congress stalls and presidents change, other actors—including states, cities, corporations, individuals, and those on the international stage—are doing what they feel is best in response to the threats posed by global warming. Some of these proceedings involve judicial challenges. Others involve states' and cities' own attempts to regulate greenhouse gases at the local level. All help to illustrate just what a president can, and cannot, achieve.

Congressional Inaction

This study of presidential power begins—as it so often does—with Congress. In the 1970s, when the study of climate change was still in its infancy, Congress enacted a series of major environmental statutes. Given the state of science at the time, climate change was not the driving force behind any of this legislation. Yet even as evidence of both the existence and the gravity of man-made global warming continued to mount in the subsequent decades, Congress failed to build on these early legislative foundations. Instead, Congress remained largely silent on the issue of climate change. As of 2017, Congress never had enacted a law expressly requiring governmental entities or private companies to lessen the impact they have on the climate.[2]

During his presidency, Obama tried hard to push Congress to take action, imploring it to send him a bill that would combat global warming. "To truly transform our economy, protect our security, and save our planet from the ravages of climate change, we need to ultimately make clean, renewable energy the profitable kind of energy," Obama told Congress in February 2009.[3]

Obama's pleas did lead to some forward movement: In June 2009, the House of Representatives managed, by a vote of 219–212, to pass a 1,400-page climate-change bill. The bill—following a cap-and-trade approach—proposed to establish emissions caps and to put in place a complex system for trading emission allowances. Yet the bill, known as the American Clean Energy and Security Act, ultimately languished in the Senate. Its final demise occurred in the summer of 2010, when Senate Majority Leader Harry Reid publicly abandoned his efforts to move the bill forward.

For Obama, who had promised to address climate change on entering the White House, the defeat of the American Clean Energy and Security Act represented a major legislative setback. Yet the bill's failure was hardly a shock. Rather, the fate of the bill fit perfectly into the overarching story that surrounds the nation's response to climate change over recent decades—a story of congressional inaction. This congressional intransigence has led critics, such as the editorial board of the *Washington Post*, to accuse Congress of taking a "head-in-the-sand approach" to climate change.[4]

A Citizen Petition

In the 1990s, various environmental activists grew tired of waiting for Congress to take action. They wanted the federal government to take affirmative steps to combat climate change, but the law gave them few points of leverage. Congress had never enacted a statute in direct response to the problem, and it did not appear prepared to do so anytime soon. As a result, the activists turned their attention to statutes that were already on the books to see if they could find some source of authority that would allow the executive branch, on its own, to begin regulating in response to climate change. The statutes they turned to included the Clean Air Act of 1970, the National Environmental Policy Act of 1969, and the Endangered Species Act of 1973. Although climate change was not the chief motivator behind any of these statutes, various environmental and conservancy groups—frustrated by Congress's more recent inaction—demanded that the executive branch find ways to deploy these preexisting statutes to address the problem.

The most noteworthy example emerged out of a citizen petition filed with the EPA in 1999 during the Clinton Administration. As we mentioned in chapter 8, a citizen petition is a mechanism, facilitated by an agency like the EPA, that allows an individual or group to argue that an agency should adopt, rescind, or change a given regulation. While the law generally allows agencies significant flexibility in deciding how to respond to petitions, the denial of a rulemaking petition can be subject to judicial review.

The citizen petition filed with the EPA in 1999 was signed by nineteen organizations, including Greenpeace USA and Friends of the Earth. Collectively, these petitioners asked the EPA to do something that it had never done before: use the authority granted to the executive branch by the Clean Air Act to regulate greenhouse gases, such as carbon dioxide (CO_2), emitted from new motor vehicles like cars and trucks.

In support of their request, the petitioners pointed to various scientific studies that demonstrated that the earth's temperature is rising and that man-made emissions of greenhouse gases are significantly accelerating this warming trend. They also documented how this warming trend poses serious risks to public health and the welfare of the planet. They cited studies showing that global warming will increase the danger of certain diseases like malaria, dengue fever, and encephalitis and that it will harm food production, air quality, water resources, wetlands, and forests.

In arguing that the EPA could address the causes of climate change, the petitioners relied on a particular provision found in the Clean Air Act that empowers the head of the EPA to make rules governing the emission of "any air pollutant" from "new motor vehicles" that "may reasonably be anticipated to endanger public health or welfare."[5] Specifically, the petitioners argued that this statutory language gives the EPA the power to regulate greenhouse gases emitted by new cars and trucks.

When the Clinton Administration's EPA received the petition in 1999, it did not respond with any sense of urgency. Instead, by January 2001, when President Bush replaced President Clinton, the EPA still had yet to rule on the petition. Before Clinton left office, however, the EPA did prepare a document that requested public comments on the issues raised. That document explained that the EPA had not yet made up its mind and wanted to hear from the public before deciding what to do.

Over the course of the next several months, the EPA (which was by then under the Bush Administration) received approximately 50,000 public comments. Yet the Bush Administration's EPA continued to sit on the petition long after the comment period closed. In fact, the EPA did not announce a ruling on the petition until 2003. When it did, the EPA denied the citizen petition and refused to regulate.

In denying the petitioners' request, the EPA offered two explanations. First, the EPA concluded that greenhouse gases are not "air pollutants" within the meaning of the Clean Air Act. In light of this conclusion, the EPA determined that Congress had not given it the statutory authority to regulate greenhouse gases. According to the EPA, in other words, the executive branch simply lacked the legal authority to do what the petitioners were asking it to do. Second, the EPA explained that even if Congress had given it the power to regulate using the Clean Air Act, it would be unwise to do so right then. To support this conclusion, the EPA claimed some residual uncertainty surrounding climate change. In addition, it argued that if it moved forward with regulating emissions from new motor vehicles, its piecemeal approach to dealing with climate change might interfere with the president's efforts to persuade other countries to sign on to a more comprehensive approach to climate change.[6]

In short, the EPA's answer to the citizen petition was a resounding no. The EPA had concluded that it could not, and should not, regulate greenhouse gases at that time. This, however, did not end the matter.

A Court Battle

When confronted with the EPA's denial, the petitioners decided to head to federal court. When they did so, they were joined by various states, including Massachusetts. This gave rise to a landmark case called *Massachusetts v. EPA*.

The case was assigned to three appellate court judges who sit in Washington, D.C., on the U.S. Court of Appeals for the D.C. Circuit. One of these judges was a Reagan appointee, one a George H.W. Bush appointee, and one a Clinton appointee. Together these three judges heard oral arguments in the case, and they reviewed lengthy written submissions. Yet, in the end, the three judges could not agree on how to handle the legal issues. So when the judges finally ruled on the case in 2005, they splintered in three different directions.

One of the judges, the Bush appointee, wrote an opinion in which

he ducked the question whether Congress gave the EPA the power to regulate greenhouse gases using the Clean Air Act. In this judge's view, even
if the Clean Air Act gave the EPA the statutory authority to regulate, the
statute clearly gave the EPA the discretion to decline to do so. The judge
noted that the question whether to regulate involved a policy determina-
tion. And the judge explained that courts will generally "uphold agency
conclusions based on policy judgments" where, as here, the "agency must
resolve issues 'on the frontiers of scientific knowledge.'"[7]

A second judge, the Clinton appointee, acknowledged that global
warming involves highly controversial questions. Yet he argued that the
case itself actually presented a very "traditional legal issue: has the Environmental Protection Agency complied with the Clean Air Act?"[8] In
answering this narrow question, the judge concluded that the EPA had
failed to comply with the statute. More specifically, the judge concluded
that Congress had indeed given the EPA the statutory power to regulate
and that the EPA had failed to provide a statutorily based justification for
refusing the petition.

The third judge, the Reagan appointee, reached an entirely different
conclusion: He argued that the case should be tossed out of federal court.
As you might remember from chapter 6, the federal courts will generally
refuse to hear cases when the challengers cannot point to some concrete,
specific harm that they have suffered. This refusal stems from a legal rule
that prohibits the federal courts from hearing cases that seek relief for
"generalized grievances"—that is, for harms that affect everyone, not just
the plaintiffs in the given case. In this third judge's view, global warming
"is harmful to humanity at large," and because of that fact, none of the
challengers could point to a specific, personalized harm that was sufficient to bring the case into federal court.[9]

Since each of the three judges preferred a different result, there was
no majority opinion. Nonetheless, in order to help the panel come to
some kind of a resolution, the third judge agreed to side with the first
judge. This meant a win for the Bush-era EPA.

However, Massachusetts and the other challengers were unwilling to take no for an answer. So they asked the U.S. Supreme Court to
weigh in, and in June 2006, the court announced that it would hear
the case. The Supreme Court then accepted legal briefs and heard

oral arguments, and in April 2007, it finally announced its decision: Massachusetts had won.

Although the court's ruling was not unanimous, five of the nine justices agreed that the EPA had not provided legally justifiable reasons for its denial of the petition. As a result, the EPA would have to go back and redo its work. The five-justice majority consisted of Justice Stevens (a Ford appointee), Justice Kennedy (a Reagan appointee), Justice Souter (a George H.W. Bush appointee), Justice Ginsburg (a Clinton appointee), and Justice Breyer (another Clinton appointee). According to these five justices, the case did not involve a generalized grievance. Rather, Massachusetts had alleged that sea levels would rise twenty to seventy centimeters by the year 2100 and that it would lose coastal land. That loss of property, according to the majority, was enough of a concrete, specific injury to enable the court to hear the matter.

This conclusion about standing allowed the court to turn next to the question of what Congress, through its enactment of the Clean Air Act decades ago, had instructed the EPA to do when faced with a citizen petition like the one filed by the plaintiffs. As to this question, the five justices reasoned that the citizen petition was correct to insist that greenhouse gases fit within the Clean Air Act's broad definition of "air pollutants." In other words, the majority concluded that Congress *had* given the EPA, via the Clean Air Act, the power to regulate greenhouse gas emissions. In addition, the majority rejected the EPA's claim that it could reject the petition because it would be unwise to regulate at that time, explaining that the EPA's reasoning was "divorced" from the statute passed by Congress.[10]

The remaining four justices joined together in dissent. This block of four consisted of Chief Justice Roberts and Justice Alito (both George W. Bush appointees), Justice Scalia (a Reagan appointee), and Justice Thomas (a George H.W. Bush appointee). Together, these dissenting justices argued that Massachusetts's alleged injury (the loss of coastal land) was highly speculative and that, as a result, the federal courts should not hear the case.

In addition, the four dissenters argued that Congress did not give the EPA the statutory power to regulate. In reaching this conclusion, the dissenters deferred to the EPA's view that the term "air pollutants," as used in the Clean Air Act, only refers to impurities in the air at the ground level or near the surface of the earth, not greenhouse gases in the "upper reaches of the atmosphere."[11]

In the end, however, the views of the minority did not prevail. Instead, the majority sent the issue back to the EPA. Notably, the Supreme Court's ruling did not go so far as to tell the EPA that it *must* use its power under the Clean Air Act to regulate greenhouse gas emissions. Rather, it told the EPA that it could not decline to regulate unless the EPA's reasons for doing so were tied in some way to the provisions of the Clean Air Act. In this sense, the decision rejected the reading of the statute advanced by the Bush Administration, which had maintained that it lacked the power to regulate greenhouse gases.

With the matter back at the EPA, the agency concluded that it was time to give the petitioners what they had been asking for. So it drafted a rule that proposed to regulate greenhouse gases, and it emailed a draft of that proposed rule to an office in the White House that is responsible for signing off on rule proposals like this one. However, the Bush White House balked. In fact, the White House tried to get the EPA to recall its email. When that effort failed, the White House simply refused to open the message. By letting the email languish in its in-box, the White House hoped to avoid a legal requirement that kicks in on receipt of such a message—namely, that it provide the public with notice that the draft rule had been sent. The White House was, in other words, doing everything it could to slow down the regulatory process.[12]

Some six months later, the *New York Times* learned of the White House's efforts to block the EPA from moving forward and ran the story.[13] Soon thereafter, Congress—exercising its power of oversight—asked the executive branch to turn over a copy of the email, as well as any related communications. The White House, however, refused to comply with Congress's oversight request. It claimed that the president had a constitutional right to reject the request,[14] and so the foot dragging continued.

Indeed, it was not until July 2008, after much back-and-forth between the EPA and the White House, that the EPA finally made some progress. However, when it did, the EPA did *not* propose a set of rules to regulate greenhouse gases. Rather, it published a document that basically told the public that the EPA was still trying to decide what to do with the citizen petition and that public comments were welcome. This move effectively enabled the Bush Administration, which was nearing the end of Bush's presidency, to run out the clock. When President Bush exited the White House in January 2009, the EPA still had not decided what to do.

Executive Action

In December 2009, nearly a year after President Obama entered the White House, the EPA finally responded to the Supreme Court's 2007 decision. It did so by issuing what is referred to as an endangerment finding. In its endangerment finding, the EPA analyzed the standards set forth in the Clean Air Act for whether an air pollutant "endangers" the public health and welfare.[15] Based on the available scientific record, the EPA concluded that greenhouse gas emissions from motor vehicles threaten public health and welfare and contribute to the dangerous buildup of climate pollution. In support of these conclusions, the EPA pointed to scientific evidence demonstrating that human emissions of greenhouse gases can lead to extreme severe storm events, such as flooding. In addition, the EPA relied on evidence demonstrating that the emissions threaten to increase the prevalence of various diseases, as well as asthma and other respiratory problems.[16]

The endangerment finding itself did not regulate greenhouse gases. However, its finalization was a big deal for two reasons. At the outset, Congress, through statute, had previously made endangerment a prerequisite to any attempt to impose greenhouse gas emissions standards for new motor vehicles under the Clean Air Act. In other words, Congress empowered the EPA to issue rules about new motor vehicles only if the EPA first demonstrates harm to public welfare. In addition, once the EPA does so, the Clean Air Act actually *requires* it to regulate.

With the endangerment finding in place, the EPA finally began the task of directly regulating greenhouse gas emissions. After undergoing extensive notice-and-comment proceedings, for example, the Obama Administration's EPA issued a final rule in May 2010 that set greenhouse gas emissions standards for light-duty vehicles, including new passenger cars, light-duty trucks, and medium-duty passenger vehicles. This was just one of several important rules that the EPA finalized in the wake of *Massachusetts*.

Perhaps the most significant rule—a rule referred to as the Clean Power Plan—came in August 2015 after a lengthy notice-and-comment rulemaking process that yielded more than 4.3 million public comments. This rule would have set the first-ever nationwide emission guidelines for states to follow in developing plans to reduce greenhouse gas emissions from power plants that are fueled by coal and other fossil fuels—emissions that accounted for about one-third of the country's greenhouse gas emissions.

President Obama called the Clean Power Plan "the single most important step America has ever taken in the fight against global climate change."[17] He predicted that, by the year 2030, the Clean Power Plan (if it were allowed to go into effect) would ensure that "carbon pollution from our power plants will be 32 percent lower than it was a decade ago."[18] That is the equivalent of taking 166 million cars off the road. [19]

As the EPA, working under Obama's supervision, was preparing to roll out its Clean Power Plan, the president was also making progress in the international arena. In early 2016, the United States and China—which together produce approximately 40 percent of all greenhouse gas emissions—jointly announced that they would sign the far-reaching Paris Climate Agreement. By the end of 2016, nearly every country in the world also had signed the agreement.

The Paris Agreement seeks to push back against the causes and effects of climate change by requiring countries joining the deal to agree to reduce their greenhouse gas emissions. It accomplishes this ambitious goal by allowing individual countries to determine how they will go about reducing their emissions. By signing onto the Paris Agreement, the Obama Administration pledged that the United States would do its best to reduce its greenhouse gas emissions by 26 to 28 percent below their 2005 levels by the year 2025. The United States would meet this ambitious goal, Obama thought, through the Clean Power Plan.

Back to Court

Not everyone in the country was pleased with the Paris Agreement, nor with the Clean Power Plan. In fact, more than two dozen states, including states like West Virginia with significant coal mining industries, promptly filed lawsuits attacking the EPA's new rule. In addition, dozens of labor unions, coal mining companies, trade groups, and other private interests filed lawsuits, arguing that the rule failed to comply with the Clean Air Act and other laws. Eventually, all the lawsuits were consolidated into one behemoth case before the U.S. Court of Appeals for the D.C. Circuit: *West Virginia v. EPA*. Joining the EPA to defend the Clean Power Plan in the case were eighteen states, six cities, and various environmental and health advocacy organizations, such as the American Lung Association. Thus, the case pitted a large swath of states that supported the Clean Power Plan against an even larger swath of states that opposed it.

Before the D.C. Circuit could decide whether the Clean Power Plan was legal, West Virginia and others asked the U.S. Supreme Court to stay—meaning to freeze—the implementation of the plan itself. A stay, they argued, would spare states and power plants from having to begin complying with the rule while the judicial branch was reviewing its legality.

The challengers' request for a stay from the Supreme Court was highly unusual. Nonetheless, on February 9, 2016, the court agreed, in a split 5–4 decision, to grant the request.[20] Chief Justice Roberts, Justice Scalia, Justice Kennedy, Justice Thomas, and Justice Alito formed the five-justice majority that voted to stay the rule and prevent the Clean Power Plan from going into effect while judicial review proceeded. Notably, just a few days later, on February 13, 2016, Justice Scalia died. This means that the court likely would have split 4–4 had it voted just a few days later. Had that occurred, the Clean Power Plan would have gone into effect while the lengthy legal proceedings unfolded.

Still, the Supreme Court's decision to stay the Clean Power Plan did not answer the central question: whether issuing the Clean Power Plan had been a legal exercise of power by the executive branch. Rather, the court's stay merely prevented the rule from going into effect while the D.C. Circuit proceeded with the review of its legality. Slowly but surely, this review took place. The D.C. Circuit accepted written briefs from the parties, and it held an astounding seven hours of oral argument on September 27, 2016. (By way of comparison, most cases argued before the D.C. Circuit receive only twenty to thirty minutes for oral arguments.) Yet by the time President Obama left the White House in January 2017, the D.C. Circuit had yet to make up its mind about how to rule in the case. This meant that the task of defending the rule in court fell to the incoming president.

Rollback

In March 2017, President Trump, flanked by coal industry workers, signed an executive order that called for a dramatic rollback of various Obama-era climate initiatives.[21] "C'mon, fellas. You know what this is? You know what this says?" Trump said to the coal miners who surrounded him while he signed the executive order. "You're going back to work."[22]

Among the many things that it did, Trump's executive order specifically directed the head of the EPA to rethink the Clean Power Plan and, if appropriate, publish for notice-and-comment new rules that would revise, suspend, or rescind the plan. Trump was not personally able to rescind the Clean Power Plan through executive order or any other means. This is because, as we discussed in chapter 3, undoing an agency's regulations generally requires that the agency itself first undergo a lengthy procedural process. A president has no legal means by which to unilaterally revoke an agency rule that already has been issued.

Still, Trump's executive order did immediately undo various orders issued by President Obama himself, including a 2013 executive order instructing the federal government to prepare for the impacts of global warming by, for example, sharing information at all levels of government and engaging in preparedness planning. It also departed from the Obama Administration's directions to agencies regarding how to calculate the social cost of carbon. Trump could order these sorts of changes because, as we have discussed, executive orders issued by one administration generally can be undone by a subsequent administration with the simple stroke of a pen.

On the same day in March that Trump signed his executive order, the EPA asked the D.C. Circuit to put on hold the pending litigation concerning the Clean Power Plan. In support of this request, it explained that it was planning to review (and possibly change or rescind) the Clean Power Plan. About a month later, the D.C. Circuit agreed to temporarily hit the pause button on its consideration of the case while the EPA figured out what it planned to do. The court then extended this waiting period further in the summer of 2017. These delays were an ominous sign for those trying to defend the Clean Power Plan. They signaled that the court might not ever move forward with a ruling in the case, given the Trump Administration's efforts to change or rescind the plan. Indeed, in the words of the *Washington Post*, the D.C. Circuit's ruling signaled a "likely end to Obama's signature climate change policy."[23]

That the Trump Administration would take steps to roll back Obama-era climate change policies did not come as a huge surprise to observers. Prior to becoming president, Trump had tweeted on several different occasions that climate change is a "hoax."[24] Once, in 2012, he even went so far as to say that the "concept of global warming was created by and for the Chinese in order to make U.S. manufacturing non-competitive."[25] Moreover, when he was on the campaign trail, Trump repeatedly promised to reduce agency regulations.

Still, the speed with which Trump sought to dismantle Obama's key climate change initiatives startled many in the global community. In particular, world leaders worried that Trump might undercut the Paris Agreement, the historic international climate change agreement that President Obama had signed less than a year before Trump took office. Given that the Paris Agreement requires countries to reduce greenhouse gas emissions, any unraveling of the EPA's Clean Power Plan would make it far more difficult for the United States to fulfill its obligations under the agreement. Indeed, in the words of the *Wall Street Journal*, "even a partial rebuke of the Clean Power Plan could make it impossible for the U.S. to accomplish what Mr. Obama pledged in the Paris deal, the capstone of his environmental legacy."[26] Moreover, given that President Obama had not sought the Senate's approval when he signed the Paris Agreement, it seemed clear that President Trump had the legal authority under U.S. law simply to withdraw from it.

After Paris

In an address from the Rose Garden on June 1, 2017, President Trump told the world that the United States would be walking away from the Paris Agreement's efforts to combat climate change. "We're getting out," he said of his intention to withdraw the United States from the Paris Agreement. "As someone who cares deeply about the environment, which I do, I cannot in good conscience support a deal that punishes the United States."[27]

Approximately four months later, the Trump Administration dealt yet another major blow to Obama's climate-change efforts: In response to Trump's March 2017 executive order, the EPA formally announced that it was launching a new notice-and-comment rulemaking proceeding to repeal the Clean Power Plan. "The Obama administration pushed the bounds of their authority so far with the [Clean Power Plan]," EPA Administrator Scott Pruitt explained. "We are committed to righting the wrongs of the Obama administration by cleaning the regulatory slate."[28]

Many Americans opposed the president's decision to withdraw from the Paris Agreement, as well as the EPA's decision to launch a rulemaking proceeding aimed at repealing the Clean Power Plan. Indeed, as the country and the world reacted to the executive branch's policy reversals, various actors across the United States announced that they would push even harder with their own efforts to respond to the challenges of climate change. These actors include private individuals, corporations, states, cities, and environmental groups. In addition, governments and actors outside the United States, and across the world, continued in their own climate-related efforts. If Trump follows through on his promise to withdraw the United States from the Paris Agreement—and if the EPA repeals the Clean Power Plan—then the efforts of these many actors likely will play an even more prominent role in combating climate change.

States such as California, for example, have worked hard for many years to respond to climate-change challenges in an effort to compensate for the federal government's failures to act. In 2006, California enacted a law known as the Global Warming Solutions Act, which requires California to lower greenhouse gas emissions to 1990 levels by the year 2020. In addition, pursuant to special powers that the Clean Air Act gives to California (and only California), the state is allowed to seek permission to set emissions standards for cars that are stricter than federal emissions standards. Other states are then permitted to adopt California's standards.[29] Efforts like these have, in a sense, turned California into a nationwide leader on issues of climate change. Yet it is not the only state taking action. In response to Trump's decision to walk away from the Paris Agreement, a coalition of more than a dozen states, which as of 2017 included not only California but also Colorado, New York, and North Carolina, quickly formed. Calling itself the U.S. Climate Alliance, this group of states has committed to reducing their emissions and to meeting the Paris Agreement target.[30]

Another prominent example of action facilitated by our country's systems of checks and balances emerges from *Juliana v. United States*, a case filed with a federal district court in Oregon. As the district court judge presiding over the case has acknowledged, the case is "no ordinary lawsuit."[31] Rather, the case pits a number of children against the executive branch of the U.S. government. These children, known as the "climate kids," argue in their lawsuit that the federal government has known for decades that CO_2 pollution causes catastrophic climate change, and that actions the executive branch has taken—or not taken—have enhanced these dangers. For example, the lawsuit points to various executive branch decisions concerning how to regulate CO_2 emissions from power plants and vehicles, as well as permitting decisions concerning fossil-fuel extraction and development on federal lands. According to the climate kids, these government decisions have deprived them of their constitutionally protected rights to life, liberty, and property and also have violated the government's obligation to hold natural resources in trust for the people and for future generations.

The climate kids first filed their lawsuit in federal court in 2015. As a result, the task of defending the federal government initially fell to the Obama Administration. Despite Obama's interest in addressing the causes of climate change, his administration was not willing to endorse all efforts at reform. And so its first move was to argue that the case should be kicked out of federal court. Specifically, Obama's lawyers argued that the case raises political rather than legal questions. In addition, they argued that the district court lacks the power to decide the case because climate change impacts "the entire planet (and all people on it) in some way."[32] According to the Obama Administration, the climate kids were therefore raising "generalized grievances," not specific, individualized injuries.

In November 2016, just days after the presidential election, the district court judge assigned to the case, Judge Ann Aiken, refused to accede to the government's request that the case be tossed out of court. Judge Aiken, a Clinton appointee, acknowledged that climate change certainly is "political" in the sense that it has "motivated partisan and sectional debate during important portions of our history."[33] However, she explained that courts can decide even politically charged cases, so long as there is law for the courts to apply. Because the climate kids were arguing that the government had deprived them of constitutional rights, Judge Aiken concluded that the case raises legal questions that the courts are well equipped to decide. "Even when a case implicates hotly contested political issues, the judiciary must not shrink from its role as a coequal branch of government," she explained.[34]

In addition, Judge Aiken rejected the Obama Administration's argument that the climate kids could not point to individualized, concrete injuries that were sufficient to bring the case into federal court. On this, the judge pointed to numerous ways that the climate kids had asserted that they have been harmed by global warming. For example, the judge placed significant weight on a declaration submitted by a thirteen-year-old girl named Jayden. In her declaration, Jayden described how a storm that ordinarily would happen only once every one thousand years flooded and destroyed her home in August 2016. According to Jayden:

> The water was flowing down the hallway, into my Mom's room and my sisters' room. The water drenched my living room and began to cover our kitchen floor. Our toilets, sinks, and bathtubs began to overflow with awful smelling sewage because our town's sewer system also flooded. Soon the sewage was everywhere. We had a stream of sewage and water running through our house.[35]

Judge Aiken looked at these and other asserted injuries, and she determined that the government's decisions had caused the climate kids concrete, individualized harm, and therefore that the case belonged in federal court.

The Trump Administration, which inherited the task of defending the federal government in the ongoing case, responded to Judge Aiken's ruling by filing a petition that sought a very rare kind of review by the U.S. Court of Appeals for the Ninth Circuit. In response, in July 2017, the Ninth Circuit agreed to pause the case temporarily pending their review of the Trump Administration's unusual request. As a result, as 2017 drew to a close, it was unclear whether the climate kids' case would ever proceed to resolution on the merits. However, regardless of the outcome, the *Juliana* lawsuit has brought even more attention to the issue of climate change. And it provides a powerful example of how individuals, even young individuals, across the United States can raise their voices and push for action.

In Sum: The Executive Branch Has Significant—but Still Limited—Power to Affect Climate-Change Policy

Climate change is one of the most serious issues facing humanity today. If Congress were to respond with legislation, it could quickly implement sweeping changes. Yet for decades, Congress has remained paralyzed.

In the wake of Congress's failure to act, concerned citizens, states, and environmental organizations, as well as the U.S. Supreme Court, have prodded the executive branch to take action. President Obama responded by pushing the executive branch to act on climate change. However, the fate of these Obama-era efforts now rests in the hands of other presidential administrations, including that of President Trump, who repeatedly has voiced his disapproval of governmental efforts to combat the threats posed by climate change.

For those interested in policies surrounding climate change, there are many developments to watch out for. Observers might keep an eye on what happens in the international arena. They also might be on the lookout for any proposed changes to key climate-change regulations. In the world of regulation, it is important to remember that, as we discussed in chapter 3, everyone has the opportunity to go to www.regulations.gov

and file comments on critical agency rulemaking proceedings.

Finally, it is important not to forget the vital role that many actors—including states, localities, interest groups, and even individual people—can play in helping to respond to environmental challenges.

Through litigation, rulemaking participation, and other forms of engagement, interest groups and states can affect climate-change policies, either in favor of increased regulation or against it. If enough voters and concerned citizens make their views known, it also is possible that more states—or perhaps even Congress—could be convinced to follow California's lead and tackle the challenges of climate change more rigorously. These possibilities reflect our systems of checks and balances at work.

Whatever one thinks about these issues, it is critical to recognize what this examination of climate-change policy confirms about presidential power: that while the president has enormous power to shape policy in this area, as in so many others, he can rarely accomplish major change all on his own. Rather, there are meaningful ways for a whole range of actors—including all of us—to play a role in helping either to advance or slow down the president's agenda.

CHAPTER 10

Ways to Get Involved

And so, my fellow Americans: ask not what your country can do for you—ask what you can do for your country.

— President John F. Kennedy speaking at his inauguration in January 1961[1]

The President of the United States has a great deal of power. Yet that power has real limits. This is due in large part to our country's complicated system of checks and balances. As a result of these constraints, every single one of us potentially has the power to affect—positively or negatively—the president's ability to advance his agenda. For those who would like to make their mark on what the president does, and how he does it, there are numerous ways to get involved. We conclude this book with a discussion of some of the most effective.

Stay Informed

Effective participation in government requires a strong understanding of how the government works. Reading books like this one—books written by experts, seeking to explain foundational concepts—is an excellent start. If you find a resource to be particularly informative, tell others about it and help them to stay informed as well.

Equally important is staying abreast of ongoing developments in government. While there is no need to follow the news obsessively, it is essential that you receive your information from reputable sources. Paying for your news (through print or online subscriptions that help to fund reliable journalism) is a great way to gain access and stay informed. It is also an important step in promoting positive change and ensuring that the media can continue to hold presidents accountable to their constituents.

Put Pressure on Your Representatives in Congress

Most of what the president wants to accomplish depends, in one way or another, on Congress. As a result, you can have an effect on presidential politics by reaching out to your representatives in Congress and letting *them* know how you want them to respond to the president's agenda. Perhaps you support new legislation that will facilitate a president's efforts. Or perhaps you oppose a recent nominee to a high-ranking governmental position. Whatever the case, tell your representatives how you feel. Start by figuring out who your representatives are. You have one representative in the U.S. House of Representatives and two in the Senate. Once you identify your representatives, you can call or email their offices to let them know what steps you would like them to take. A website such as www.callmycongress.com can help you find this information.

You also might consider attending town hall meetings hosted by your representatives and speaking up there to express your views. Or you might submit op-eds, directed to your representatives, to your local newspapers. When enough people put this sort of pressure on members of Congress, they usually do respond. And, of course, if you are eligible to vote, be sure to exercise your right to vote in *every* election, including those for congressional office.

Get Involved in State and Local Government

As we explained in chapter 7, state and local politics really do matter. Among other things, state and local governments possess a great deal of power to support or push back against a president's agenda. You can take advantage of this dynamic by getting involved. Again, you will need to do a bit of research. Figure out how your state and local governments are structured, and who your representatives are. Then, tell those representatives what you would like them to do, including whether to support or resist various aspects of the president's agenda. You might accomplish this by attending public meetings or by calling their offices. You could even consider running for office yourself. And, again, if you are eligible, vote in every election—national, state, and local, primary and general, regularly scheduled and special.

Support Interest Groups Working Toward Your Desired Outcomes

Supporting an interest group—the right interest group for you—can be one of the most effective means through which to advance your preferred agenda. These groups often form for the very purpose of exerting pressure on powerful actors, including the president. If you are able to identify a well-organized and effective interest group that shares your beliefs and priorities, consider making it a real priority to support that group. Many of the most successful of these groups employ scores of full-time professionals, whose employment gives them the time and resources they need to push for change, whether through lobbying, litigation, or other important means. You will want to focus on interest groups that track your own preferred agendas and ideologies. Successful interest groups generally on the more liberal side include the American Civil Liberties Union and the National Resources Defense Council. Successful interest groups generally on the more conservative side include the National Rifle Association and the American Conservative Union. Across the ideological spectrum, there are many, many more groups that have the ability to make a real difference in national politics. Most of these groups rely heavily on the support of their members. Consider supporting or becoming a member of groups that share your vision.

Support Politicians and Parties Working Toward Your Desired Outcomes

Political parties, as well as politicians, rely on the work of constituents to help with organizing, reaching out to voters, and forming their own views on legislation and other policy questions. Consider joining your local branch of a political party and helping that party grow in ways you think are appropriate. Alternatively (or in addition), consider volunteering on behalf of one of your representatives, either with campaign-related work or with the actual business of governing.

Speak Up!

Exercise your First Amendment right to free speech and speak out—either in support of or against a president's agenda. Consider taking these efforts a step further by visiting the website www.regulations.gov and submitting a comment on pending regulations. By law, agencies must consider all significant comments that they receive. If you take this step, remember that rulemaking is not a vote-counting process. Instead, agencies must make rulemaking decisions based on statutorily relevant factual, legal, and policy considerations. As a result, the most effective comments are detailed and well supported and do more than simply express support for or opposition to a proposed rule. To help ensure the effectiveness of your individual comments, consider consulting various online resources—such as those provided in the endnote that accompanies this sentence—that provide helpful tips for drafting comments.[2]

In addition, consider composing a citizen petition that asks an agency to regulate or to deregulate something you know and care about. Again, various online resources provide helpful tips that you might consult before drafting a citizen petition.[3] More generally, be sure to exercise your constitutionally conferred right to free speech in the ways you feel are appropriate—perhaps by submitting editorials to newspapers or blogs, joining peaceful protests, or simply reaching out to others.

For Every Eligible Voter, Vote in All Elections

Presidential elections are important. Yet to make a real, lasting impact, voters need to vote in all elections. Even if your preferred candidate is elected president, he will have an exceedingly difficult time getting things done if other governmental actors—including members of Congress and state and local officials—are allied against him. By extension, even if your preferred presidential candidate loses the election, you can still have real influence by helping to vote others into office. Unfortunately, voting is not always convenient and easy. (To that end, consider petitioning your state representatives for appropriate reforms in voting laws, or looking into volunteer opportunities during elections, to help make voting easier for others.) Despite the challenges associated with voting, every eligible voter should make a concerted effort to vote in every single election.

Encourage New Generations of Americans to Learn About—and Protect—Our Government

Democratic governments do not sustain themselves. Instead, democracies like ours are kept alive by informed citizens—citizens who work to gain the knowledge necessary to actively participate in government and to protect the system of checks and balances built into our constitutional structure. Sandra Day O'Connor, a retired U.S. Supreme Court justice, has recognized as much. "The practice of democracy is not passed down through the gene pool," she has explained. "It must be taught and learned anew by each generation of citizens."[4] If you have children, grandchildren, or other young people in your family, talk to them about our nation's complex system of government. Teach them about the importance of voting, the rule of law, and civic engagement. Various online resources might provide you with ideas for how to make these discussions fun and engaging. For example, iCivics (www.icivics.org), an organization founded by Justice O'Connor, provides free online educational video games designed to help young people understand how our government works.

. . .

This list of suggestions will get you far—but it is just a start. There are many other ways to participate in the process, including through community outreach and education, by voting with your wallet (that is, by directing your spending toward businesses that support your preferred policies), or even just by taking the time to talk through political issues with your friends and family. Regardless of what you choose to do, it is important to remember that there *is* the potential for your civic participation to matter, even when it comes to something as big as presidential politics.

The president's power is vast, but it is far from unlimited. His ability to get things done depends on many other people—including on people like you.

Online Resources

Those interested in diving more deeply into the law of presidential power can take advantage of many excellent online resources. Among these resources is a website on presidential power that is maintained by the Gallagher Law Library at the University of Washington School of Law. It is available at http://guides.lib.uw.edu/law/prespower/reference. Below are a few more of our favorite resources.

The U.S. Supreme Court
www.scotusblog.com
www.oyez.org

The Regulatory Process
www.regulations.gov
www.federalregister.gov
www.theregreview.org

Legal Blogs
www.takecareblog.com
www.lawfareblog.com
www.concurringopinions.com

Civics Education
www.icivics.org

Endnotes

INTRODUCTION

1 RICHARD E. NEUSTADT, PRESIDENTIAL POWER AND THE MODERN PRESIDENTS: THE POLITICS OF LEADERSHIP FROM ROOSEVELT TO REAGAN 10 (1990).

2 *Donald Trump's Entire Republican Convention Speech*, CNN, https://goo.gl/c6ckVh.

3 In the interest of disclosure, we note that, at various stages of the *Washington v. Trump* litigation, lawyers for the State of Washington consulted with the authors of this book.

4 *See* Washington v. Trump, No. C17-0141JLR, 2017 WL 462040 (W.D. Wash. Feb. 3, 2017).

5 Donald J. Trump (@realDonaldTrump), TWITTER (Feb. 4, 2017, 5:12 AM), https://perma.cc/QLU2-Q7VJ.

6 DONALD J. TRUMP, DONALD TRUMP'S CONTRACT WITH THE AMERICAN VOTER (2016), https://perma.cc/2TF7-NSME.

7 *See* Sanford Levinson & Jack M. Balkin, *Constitutional Crises*, 157 U. PA. L. REV. 707, 711 (2009).

8 U.S. CONST. art. II, § 1.

9 Univision News, *Transcript: President Obama's Interview with Univision*, ABC NEWS (Jan. 31, 2013), https://perma.cc/PRZ4-TBTC.

10 3 THE RECORDS OF THE FEDERAL CONVENTION OF 1787, at 85 (Max Farrand ed., 1911), https://perma.cc/4WVT-EG8M.

CHAPTER 1

1 ADAMS-JEFFERSON LETTERS: THE COMPLETE CORRESPONDENCE BETWEEN THOMAS JEFFERSON AND ABIGAIL AND JOHN ADAMS 463 (Lester J. Cappon ed., 1987).

2 THE FEDERALIST NO. 47 (James Madison).

3 *See* William A. Galston, *Why the 2005 Social Security Initiative Failed, and What It Means for the Future*, BROOKINGS (Sept. 21, 2007), https://perma.cc/DLD7-8Q8K.

4 Exec. Order No. 13492, 74 Fed. Reg. 4897, 4898 (Jan. 22, 2009).

5 *Marbury v. Madison*, 5 U.S. 137, 163 (1803).

6   PBS NewsHour, *Former Supreme Court Justice Souter on The Danger of America's 'Pervasive Civic Ignorance,'* YouTube (Sept. 17, 2012), https://goo.gl/UZW82n.

7   *See, e.g.*, Ted Barrett, *61 Senators Sign Letter to Preserve Filibuster Rules*, CNN (Apr. 9, 2017), https://goo.gl/8RG3Hk.

8   *See* U.S. Senate Historical Office, *March 2, 1805: Indicted Vice President Bids Senate Farewell*, https://goo.gl/GNsgtK.

9   *See* Barrett, *supra* note 7.

10 THE FEDERALIST NO. 52 (James Madison). There is some dispute over whether James Madison or Alexander Hamilton wrote this paper.

11 JULIE JENNINGS, CONG. RESEARCH SERV., R43590, FEDERAL WORKFORCE STATISTICS SOURCES: OPM AND OMB 1 (2016), http://perma.cc/4PPT-7ZYN.

12 U.S. CONST. art. II, § 1.

13 *But see, e.g.*, U.S. CONST. amend XII (describing the role that the vice president plays in tallying votes cast for president and vice president); U.S. CONST. amend XXV (describing the role that the vice president plays when the president is "unable to discharge the powers and duties of his office").

14 U.S. Term Limits, Inc. v. Thornton, 514 U.S. 779, 838 (1995) (Kennedy, J., concurring).

15 *Id.*

16 *See* U.S. CONST. amend. X.

17 *See* U.S. CONST. art. VI, cl. 2 ("This Constitution, and the Laws of the United States which shall be made in Pursuance thereof; and all Treaties made, or which shall be made, under the Authority of the United States, shall be the supreme Law of the Land . . . .").

18 *Cf.* Geier v. Am. Honda Motor Co., 529 U.S. 861 (2000).

19 *See, e.g.*, Wyeth v. Levine, 555 U.S. 555 (2009).

20 West Virginia State Bd. of Educ. v. Barnette, 319 U.S. 624, 638 (1943).

CHAPTER 2

1   *Youngstown Sheet & Tube Company v. Sawyer*, 343 U.S. 579, 585 (1952).

2   *See id.*

3   Exec. Order No. 10,340, 3 C.F.R. 861 (1949–1953).

4   Patricia L. Bellia, *The Story of the* Steel Seizure *Case*, *in* PRESIDENTIAL POWERS STORIES 233, 243 (Christopher H. Schroeder & Curtis A. Bradley eds., 2009).

5   *Youngstown*, 343 U.S. at 585.

6   *Id.* at 634 (Jackson, J., concurring).

7   In addition to invoking the Constitution and statutes, presidents sometimes point
    to a third source of presidential power: so-called "inherent power." Inherent powers
    are not necessarily grounded in either the Constitution or in a particular statute.
    This category of presidential power is quite controversial, and legal scholars have
    heavily debated whether it even exists. This third source of presidential power
    generally applies, if at all, in the area of foreign affairs.

8   U.S. CONST. art. II, § 3.

9   *See* U.S. CONST. art. I, § 1 ("All legislative Powers herein granted shall be vested
    in a Congress of the United States, which shall consist of a Senate and House of
    Representatives.").

10 U.S. CONST. art. II, § 3.

11 Robert Pear, *Clinton's Health Plan: The Overview; Congress Is Given Clinton
    Proposal for Health Care*, N.Y. TIMES (Oct. 28, 1993), https://goo.gl/KMkn4c.

12 John F. Kennedy, *Radio and Television Report to the American People on Civil Rights*,
    in PUBLIC PAPERS OF THE PRESIDENTS OF THE UNITED STATES:
    JOHN F. KENNEDY 1963, at 469 (1964).

13 RICHARD E. NEUSTADT, PRESIDENTIAL POWER AND THE MODERN PRESIDENTS:
    THE POLITICS OF LEADERSHIP FROM ROOSEVELT TO REAGAN 29–32 (1990).

14 U.S. CONST. art. I, § 7, cl. 2 (setting forth the veto power).

15 *Vetoes*, U.S. SENATE, https://perma.cc/P8X6-QSFD.

16 *See* Clinton v. City of New York, 524 U.S. 417, 421 (1998) (holding the Line Item
    Veto Act unconstitutional).

17 *See generally Presidential Signing Statements*, LIBR. OF CONGRESS,
    https://perma.cc/4JTY-8VTR.

18 *See* Grover Cleveland, *February 16, 1887: Veto of Texas Seed Bill*, UVA: MILLER
    CTR., https://perma.cc/M4GY-7RB5.

19 *Id.*

20 *Id.*

21 *See* U.S. CONST. art. I, § 7, cl. 3.

22 BENJAMIN GINSBERG, PRESIDENTIAL GOVERNMENT 205 (2016).

23 *See* 18 CONG. REC. 1875–76 (1887).

24 U.S. CONST. art. II, § 2, cl. 2 ("[The President] shall nominate, and by and
    with the Advice and Consent of the Senate, shall appoint Ambassadors, other public
    Ministers and Consuls, Judges of the supreme Court, and all other Officers of the
    United States, whose Appointments are not herein otherwise provided for, and
    which shall be established by Law . . . .").

25 *Id.* ("[T]he Congress may by Law vest the Appointment of such inferior Officers,
    as they think proper, in the President alone, in the Courts of Law, or in the Heads
    of Departments.").

26 *Id.*

27 Christopher M. Davis & Michael Greene, Cong. Research Serv., RL30959, Presidential Appointee Positions Requiring Senate Confirmation and Committees Handling Nominations 41–42 (2017), https://perma.cc/2BL6-WJ7W.

28 Some legal scholars have argued that the Constitution implicitly allows other forms of removal for judges. *See* Saikrishna Prakash & Steven D. Smith, *How To Remove a Federal Judge*, 116 Yale L.J. 72 (2006). However, "[t]he conventional wisdom is to the contrary." John F. Manning, *Separation of Powers as Ordinary Interpretation*, 124 Harv. L. Rev. 1939, 1982 n.221 (2011) (citing contrary authorities). In any event, there is no precedent for removing an Article III judge outside of the impeachment process.

29 13 Annals of Cong. 353 (1804).

30 Free Enter. Fund v. Pub. Co. Accounting Oversight Bd., 561 U.S. 477, 514 (2010).

31 Federal Trade Commission Act, Pub. L. 63-203, § 1, 38 Stat. 717, 718 (1914) (codified as amended at 15 U.S.C. § 41 (2012)).

32 Humphrey's Ex'r v. United States, 295 U.S. 602, 632 (1935).

33 *See, e.g.*, Morrison v. Olson, 487 U.S. 654 (1988).

34 Jonathan H. Adler, Opinion, *Acting Attorney General Orders Justice Department Attorneys Not to Defend Immigration Executive Order*, Wash. Post (Jan. 30, 2017), https://goo.gl/f6LMZZ.

35 *Id.*

36 Despite the prevailing view that a president may not use his removal power to commit a crime, there does remain some disagreement. *See, e.g.*, Richard H. Pildes, *In the View of the Supreme Court, Alan Dershowitz Is Wrong About the Powers of the President*, Lawfare (June 9, 2017, 12:52 PM), https://perma.cc/2PWU-TEUK (describing—and criticizing—the contrary view); Charlie Savage, *Can Presidents Obstruct Justice? The Latest Trump Fight, Explained*, N.Y. Times (Dec. 4, 2017), https://goo.gl/uVDaue.

37 *See, e.g.*, 18 U.S.C. § 1512(c)(2) (2012); *see also supra* note 36 (discussing conflicting views).

38 U.S. Const. art. II, § 1, cl. 1 ("The executive Power shall be vested in a President of the United States of America."); U.S. Const. art. II, § 3 (providing that the President shall "take Care that the Laws be faithfully executed").

39 *See generally* Fair Labor Standards Act of 1938, 29 U.S.C. §§ 201–219 (2012).

40 *Id.* § 213(d).

41 *See* 29 C.F.R. 570.124 (2016).

42 *See* Memorandum from Janet Napolitano, Sec'y, U.S. Dep't of Homeland Sec., to David V. Aguilar, Acting Comm'r, U.S. Customs & Border Prot., et al. (June 15, 2012), https://perma.cc/SV8Z-A2L8.

43 *See generally* Remarks on Immigration Reform and an Exchange with Reporters, 1 Pub. Papers 800 (June 15, 2012), https://perma.cc/ULD5-STYX.

44 *See* William P. Marshall, *Eleven Reasons Why Presidential Power Inevitably Expands and Why It Matters*, 88 B.U. L. Rev. 505, 509–10 (2008).

45 U.S. Const. art. II, § 2, cl. 1 ("The President shall be Commander in Chief of the Army and Navy of the United States, and of the Militia of the several States, when called into the actual Service of the United States.").

46 *Youngstown*, 343 U.S. at 641–42 (Jackson, J., concurring) (describing the views of others) (emphasis added).

47 *See, e.g.*, Michael D. Ramsey & Stephen I. Vladeck, *Commander in Chief Clause*, Nat'l Const. Ctr., https://goo.gl/m7BeiX.

48 Charlie Savage, *2 Top Lawyers Lost to Obama in Libya War Policy Debate*, N.Y. Times (June 17, 2011), https://goo.gl/J7JTMm.

49 *Youngstown*, 343 U.S. at 637 (Jackson, J., concurring).

50 *See* U.S. Const. art. I, § 8. In addition, the Constitution gives Congress the power to "grant Letters of Marque and Reprisal," to "make Rules concerning Captures on Land and Water," and to "make Rules for the Government and Regulation of the land and naval Forces," among other related powers. *Id.*

51 Authorization for Use of Military Force, Pub. L. No. 107-40, § 2(a), 115 Stat. 224, 224 (2001).

52 *See* War Powers Resolution, Pub. L. No. 93-148, 87 Stat. 555 (codified as amended at 50 U.S.C. §§ 1541–48 (2012)).

53 Restricting First Use of Nuclear Weapons Act of 2017, H.R. 669, 115th Cong. (2017).

54 *See Treaties*, U.S. Senate, https://perma.cc/LUN9-T8GG.

55 *See* Tanya Somanader, *President Obama: The United States Formally Enters the Paris Agreement*, White House (Sept. 3, 2016), https://perma.cc/MB88-A37C.

56 42 U.S.C. § 7409(b)(1) (2012).

57 *See, e.g.*, United States v. Grimaud, 220 U.S. 506 (1911).

58 *See* Whitman v. Am. Trucking Ass'ns, 531 U.S. 457 (2001).

59 *See* Occupational Safety and Health Act of 1970, Pub. L. 91-596, § 3, 84 Stat. 1590, 1591 (codified as amended at 29 U.S.C. § 652(8) (2012)) (requiring that workplace safety and health standards be "reasonably necessary or appropriate to provide safe or healthful employment").

60 Occupational Exposure to Respirable Crystalline Silica, 81 Fed. Reg. 16,286 (Mar. 25, 2016) (codified at 29 C.F.R. pts. 1910, 1915, 1926 (2016)).

CHAPTER 3

1 Rebecca Savransky, *Obama to Trump: 'What Magic Wand Do You Have?,'* HILL (June 1, 2016), https://perma.cc/KM4S-WS8V.

2 *Obama on Executive Actions: 'I've Got a Pen and I've Got a Phone,'* CBS DC (Jan. 14, 2014), https://perma.cc/Z8BB-7BD9.

3 *See* 160 CONG. REC. H1474 (daily ed. Jan. 28, 2014) (President Obama's State of the Union).

4 *See generally A Year of Action,* WHITE HOUSE, https://perma.cc/4PG2-3ZJD.

5 U.S. CONST. art. II, § 3.

6 Other forms of unilateral executive directives issued by presidents, such as those labeled "presidential memoranda," tend to have the same principal purpose—that is, to give the president a formal way of telling executive branch officials what to do.

7 *See generally* KENNETH R. MAYER, WITH THE STROKE OF A PEN: EXECUTIVE ORDERS AND PRESIDENTIAL POWER (2001).

8 For helpful discussions of executive orders, see generally *id.*, and Erica Newland, Note, *Executive Orders in Court,* 124 YALE L.J. 2026 (2015).

9 As explained in note 7 of chapter 2, presidents have at times argued that they are empowered to act based on authorities that are not necessarily derived from either the Constitution or statute. However, this theory is limited in its potential application and highly contested.

10 *See* MAYER, *supra* note 7 at 51.

11 *See* U.S. CONST. art. II, § 2, cl. 1 (expressly allowing the president to request the "Opinion, in writing, of the principal Officer in each of the executive Departments, upon any Subject relating to the Duties of their respective Offices").

12 Exec. Order No. 9981, 3 C.F.R. 722 (1943–1948).

13 Exec. Order No. 11,478, 3 C.F.R. 803 (1966–1970), *reprinted as amended in* 42 U.S.C. § 2000e note (2012).

14 *See, e.g.,* Exec. Order No. 13,087, 3 C.F.R. 191 (1999), *reprinted as amended in* 42 U.S.C. § 2000e note (2012) (protecting federal government workers from employment discrimination based on sexual orientation).

15 Exec. Order No. 13,658, 79 Fed. Reg. 9851 (Feb. 12, 2014).

16 Often these sorts of orders—orders that regulate private individuals and that reach outside of the government—are labeled proclamations rather than executive orders.

17 Although the order in question was labeled a proclamation, *see supra* note 16, rather than an executive order, this label did not affect how the Supreme Court analyzed its legality.

18 United States v. Curtiss-Wright Exp. Corp., 299 U.S. 304 (1936).

19 *See* Chamber of Commerce v. Reich, 74 F.3d 1322 (D.C. Cir. 1996).

20 Francesca Chambers, *Trump Takes the Ax to Obamacare with His First Oval Office Order: He Signs Directive Making Explicit He WILL Repeal and Replace*, DAILY MAIL (Jan. 20, 2017), https://goo.gl/7R8mzp.

21 Julie Hirschfeld Davis & Robert Pear, *Trump Issues Executive Order Scaling Back Parts of Obamacare*, N.Y. TIMES (Jan. 20, 2017), https://goo.gl/vis7dA.

22 Exec. Order No. 13,765, 82 Fed. Reg. 8,351 (Jan. 20, 2017) (emphasis added).

23 *Id.*

24 *See* Kathryn A. Watts, *Controlling Presidential Control*, 114 MICH. L. REV. 683, 727 (2016). *See generally* Kevin M. Stack, *The President's Statutory Powers to Administer the Law*, 106 COLUM. L. REV. 263 (2006).

25 Exec. Order No. 12,291, 3 C.F.R. 127 (1982).

26 *See* Elizabeth G. Porter & Kathryn A. Watts, *Visual Rulemaking*, 91 N.Y.U. L. REV. 1183, 1221 (2016).

27 *See, e.g.*, Elena Kagan, *Presidential Administration*, 114 HARV. L. REV. 2245 (2001); Peter L. Strauss, Foreword, *Overseer, or "The Decider"? The President in Administrative Law*, 75 GEO. WASH. L. REV. 696 (2007).

28 U.S. CONST. art. II, § 3.

29 *See generally* Kagan, *supra* note 27.

30 GARY LAWSON, FEDERAL ADMINISTRATIVE LAW 5 (7th ed. 2016).

31 *See* Administrative Procedure Act, 5 U.S.C. § 553 (2012).

32 *See, e.g.*, Portland Cement Ass'n v. Ruckelshaus, 486 F.2d 375, 393 (D.C. Cir. 1973) ("It is not consonant with the purpose of a rule-making proceeding to promulgate rules on the basis of ... data that, [to a] critical degree, is known only to the agency.").

33 *See, e.g.*, Reytblatt v. U.S. Nuclear Regulatory Comm'n, 105 F.3d 715, 722 (D.C. Cir. 1997) ("An agency need not address every comment, but it must respond in a reasoned manner to those that raise significant problems.").

34 For those who are visually inclined, a useful chart illustrating the notice-and-comment process can be found online. *See Reg Map*, REGINFO.GOV, https://perma.cc/WYX9-3R7W.

35 *See, e.g.*, Motor Vehicles Mfrs. Ass'n v. State Farm Mut. Auto. Ins. Co., 463 U.S. 29 (1983).

36 *See* Nina A. Mendelson, *Disclosing "Political" Oversight of Agency Decision Making*, 108 MICH. L. REV. 1127, 1143 (2010); Kathryn A. Watts, *Proposing a Place for Politics in Arbitrary and Capricious Review*, 119 YALE L.J. 2, 53–58 (2009).

37 *See* The President's News Conference, 2 PUB. PAPERS 1237 (Aug. 10, 1995) (announcing that "by executive authority, I will restrict sharply the advertising, promotion, distribution, and marketing of cigarettes to teenagers").

38 Frank James, *Clinton Declares War on Smoking by Children*, CHI. TRIB. (Aug. 24, 1996), https://perma.cc/PY3Q-QNJ9; *see also* Remarks Announcing the Final Rule to Protect Youth from Tobacco, 2 PUB. PAPERS 1332, 1332–34 (Aug. 23, 1996).

39 FDA v. Brown & Williamson Tobacco Corp., 529 U.S. 120, 125 (2000).

40 *Id.* at 126.

41 Family Smoking Prevention and Tobacco Control Act, Pub. L. No. 111-31, 123 Stat. 1776 (2009) (codified as amended in scattered sections of 5, 15, and 21 U.S.C.).

42 *See, e.g., Donald Trump's Entire Republican Convention Speech*, CNN, https://goo.gl/e9YzAf.

43 Memorandum on the Fiduciary Duty Rule, 2017 DAILY COMP. PRES. DOC. 1–2 (Feb. 3, 2017).

44 Exec. Order No. 13,772, 82 Fed. Reg. 9965 (Feb. 3, 2017).

45 Exec. Order No. 13,778, 82 Fed. Reg. 12,497 (Feb. 28, 2017).

46 *See* Remarks at the American Center for Mobility in Ypsilanti Township, Michigan, 2017 DAILY COMP. PRES. DOC. 2–3 (Mar. 15, 2017).

47 Exec. Order No. 13,771, 82 Fed. Reg. 9339 (Jan. 30, 2017).

48 *See* Scott Greenberg, *Federal Tax Laws and Regulations Are Now Over 10 Million Words Long*, TAX FOUND. (Oct. 8, 2015), https://perma.cc/3M99-BS4U.

49 *See* U.S. DEP'T OF THE TREASURY, PUB. NO. 55B, INTERNAL REVENUE SERVICE DATA BOOK, 2014 (2015), https://perma.cc/6CZL-GLV7.

50 *See* Exec. Order No. 13,768, 82 Fed. Reg. 8799 (Jan. 25, 2017).

51 *See* Heckler v. Chaney, 470 U.S. 821 (1985).

52 *See* 159 CONG. REC. H446 (daily ed. Feb. 12, 2013) (President Obama's State of the Union).

53 *See* Address to the Nation on Immigration Reform, 2014 DAILY COMP. PRES. DOC. 2 (Nov. 20, 2014).

54 *'This Week' Transcript: Ben Carson and Speaker Paul Ryan*, ABC NEWS (Nov. 1, 2015), https://perma.cc/57WR-FTQL.

55 *See* United States v. Texas, 136 S. Ct. 2271 (2016) (mem.), *aff'g* 787 F.3d 733 (5th Cir. 2015); *see also* Texas v. United States, 86 F. Supp. 3d 591 (S.D. Tex. 2015).

CHAPTER 4

1 Andy Barr, *The GOP's No-Compromise Pledge*, POLITICO (Oct. 28, 2010), http://perma.cc/3VDK-RDHB.

2 Robert Ajemian, *Where Is the Real George Bush?*, TIME, Jan. 26, 1987, at 20, https://2.gl/m27Xj2.

3 Margaret Garrard Warner, *Bush Battles the 'Wimp Factor,'* NEWSWEEK, Oct. 19, 1987, at 28–29, http://perma.cc/RSK7-N4UQ.

4 Republican National Convention, *Acceptance Speech, President George H.W. Bush, 1988 Republican National Convention*, YOUTUBE (Mar. 7, 2016), https://goo.gl/B6GNBx.

5   *See* U.S. CONST. art. I, § 1 ("All legislative Powers herein granted shall be vested in a Congress of the United States, which shall consist of a Senate and House of Representatives.").

6   Statement on Signing the Countering America's Adversaries Through Sanctions Act, 2017 DAILY COM. PRES. DOC. 1 (Aug. 2, 2017), https://perma.cc/G2T9-H88K.

7   U.S. CONST. art. I, § 7, cl. 3.

8   103 CONG. REC. 16,263–456 (1957) (statement of Sen. Thurmond), https://perma.cc/8QFC-T3HH.

9   Dana Milbank, Opinion, *Ted Cruz's Phony Obamacare Filibuster Was Really About … Ted Cruz*, WASH. POST (Sept. 25, 2013), https://goo.gl/dJajH4.

10   Victoria Walker, *Trump Says He Will Build 'Impenetrable, Physical, Tall, Powerful, Beautiful' Border*, WASH. POST (Aug. 31, 2016), https://goo.gl/xkvgEw.

11   The White House, *President Trump Delivers Remarks at the Department of Homeland Security*, YOUTUBE (Jan. 25, 2017), https://goo.gl/kRmm2j.

12   Reuters, *Immediate Construction of Trump's Wall Hits a Financial Roadblock*, NEWSWEEK (Mar. 1, 2017), http://perma.cc/8PME-BDWX.

13   OFFICE OF MGMT. & BUDGET, EXEC. OFFICE OF THE PRESIDENT, AMERICA FIRST: A BUDGET BLUEPRINT TO MAKE AMERICA GREAT AGAIN (2017), http://perma.cc/MDP5-GDLB.

14   *See* Caitlin Dickson, *Marijuana Shops Outnumber Starbucks in Denver*, ATLANTIC (July 6, 2011), http://perma.cc/3PT9-NZL9.

15   Consolidated and Further Continuing Appropriations Act of 2015, Pub. L. No. 113-235, § 538, 128 Stat. 2130, 2217 (2014).

16   *See generally* United States v. McIntosh, 833 F.3d 1163 (9th Cir. 2016).

17   *See, e.g.*, Train v. City of New York, 420 U.S. 35, 39–41 (1975) (describing a dispute over spending associated with the Federal Water Pollution Control Act Amendments of 1972).

18   *See, e.g.*, Guste v. Brinegar, 388 F. Supp. 1319, 1324–25 (D.D.C. 1975); *cf.* Train v. City of New York, 420 U.S. 35 (1975).

19   Linda Greenhouse, *Bork's Nomination Is Rejected, 58–42; Reagan 'Saddened,'* N.Y. TIMES (Oct. 24, 1987), https://goo.gl/BgrNjF.

20   133 Cong. Rec. 18,519 (1987) (statement of Sen. Kennedy).

21   Michael Oreskes, *Senate Rejects Tower, 53-47; First Cabinet Veto Since '59; Bush Confers on New Choice*, N.Y. TIMES (Mar. 10, 1989), https://goo.gl/h9f8dD.

22   Eastland v. United States Servicemen's Fund, 421 U.S. 491, 504 n.15 (1975) (internal quotation marks omitted).

23   *See* DOUGLAS L. KRINER & ERIC SCHICKLER, INVESTIGATING THE PRESIDENT: CONGRESSIONAL CHECKS ON PRESIDENTIAL POWER 7 (2016).

24   *See id.* at 3.

25 U.S. CONST. art. II, § 4.

26 *Id.* amend. XXV, § 1.

27 *Id.* amend. XXV, §§ 3–4.

28 *Id.* amend. XXV, § 4.

CHAPTER 5

1   *Clinton: Being President Like Being Cemetery Superintendent,* NBC NEWS
    (Feb. 25, 2014), https://goo.gl/qgZY7i.

2   JULIE JENNINGS, CONG. RESEARCH SERV., R43590, FEDERAL WORKFORCE
    STATISTICS SOURCES: OPM AND OMB 1 (2016), http://perma.cc/4PPT-7ZYN.

3   Katie Reilly, *Rick Perry Infamously Forgot About the Department of Energy.
    Now He Might Lead It,* TIME (Dec. 12, 2016), https://goo.gl/GeSTBi.

4   See U.S. DEP'T OF ENERGY, DOE/CF-0090, FY 2014 CONGRESSIONAL BUDGET
    REQUEST: BUDGET HIGHLIGHTS 13–14 (2013), http://perma.cc/TH2G-MUWN;
    U.S. OFFICE OF PERS. MGMT., PPA-02900-06-17, SIZING UP THE EXECUTIVE
    BRANCH: FISCAL YEAR 2016, at 6 tbl.3 (2017), http://perma.cc/KV7E-AQK9; U.S.
    DEP'T OF ENERGY, DOE/CF-0067, STRATEGIC PLAN: 2014–2018, at 1 (2014),
    https://perma.cc/F3X8-AHBE.

5   *Offices,* U.S. DEP'T OF ENERGY, http://perma.cc/MZ55-SGCM.

6   John M. Kamensky, *Mapping the Contours of the Federal Government,* ADMIN.
    & REG. L. NEWS, Spring 2013, at 3, http://perma.cc/HWP2-XKMM.

7   *See* John M. Broder, *Re-Election Strategy Is Tied to a Shift on Smog,* N.Y. TIMES
    (Nov. 16, 2011), https://goo.gl/Vk6J5s.

8   *See* Josh Margolin, *EPA Chief on Verge of Quitting After Obama Rejected Pollution
    Proposal,* N.Y. POST (Sept. 19, 2011), https://perma.cc/F5DP-R4DQ.

9   Rod J. Rosenstein, Acting Attorney Gen., Dep't of Justice, Order No. 3915-2017:
    Appointment of Special Counsel to Investigate Russian Interference with the
    2016 Presidential Election and Related Matters (May 17, 2017),
    https://perma.cc/YUV4-CK3A. The special counsel was also empowered
    with limited jurisdiction to investigate other related matters. *Id.*

10 Donald J. Trump (@realDonaldTrump), TWITTER (May 18, 2017, 4:52 AM),
    https://perma.cc/F778-K9W8.

11 *See* Office of Pers. Mgmt., *Executive Branch Civilian Employment Since 1940,* OPM.
    GOV, https://perma.cc/MCL3-JN2Z.

12 *See, e.g.,* 5 U.S.C. § 2301 (2012); *see also* Office of Pers. Mgmt., *Merit System
    Principles and Performance Management,* OPM.GOV, https://perma.cc/L89F-G63U.

13 *See, e.g.,* 5 U.S.C. §§ 7323–24 (2012).

14 *See, e.g.*, 5 U.S.C. § 2301(b)(8)(A) (2012).

15 *See* Peter L. Strauss, *The Place of Agencies in Government: Separation of Powers and the Fourth Branch*, 84 COLUM. L. REV. 573, 586 (1984).

16 *See* Jon D. Michaels, *An Enduring, Evolving Separation of Powers*, 115 COLUM. L. REV. 515, 544–45 (2015).

17 *See* Jennifer Nou, *Bureaucratic Resistance from Below*, YALE J. ON REG.: NOTICE & COMMENT (Nov. 16, 2016), https://perma.cc/UN79-PNY5.

18 Another lever that civil servants could potentially try to use involves filing suit against the agency that they work for. However, when and whether the courts will allow such civil servant suits remains an open question. *See* Alex Hemmer, Note, *Civil Servant Suits*, 124 YALE L.J. 758, 761–62 (2014); *see also* Crane v. Napolitano, 920 F. Supp. 2d 724, 734–43 (N.D. Tex. 2013), *aff'd sub nom.* Crane v. Johnson, 783 F.3d 244, 247 (5th Cir. 2015).

19 *See* Gillian E. Metzger, *The Interdependent Relationship Between Internal and External Separation of Powers*, 59 EMORY L.J. 423, 445 (2009).

20 Tummino v. Torti, 603 F. Supp. 2d 519, 531 (E.D.N.Y. 2009), *amended by* Tummino v. Hamburg, Nos. 05-CV-366 (ERK)–(VVP), 12-CV-763 (ERK)–(VVP), 2013 WL 865851 (E.D.N.Y. Mar. 6, 2013). For a thorough history of the FDA's handling of Plan B, see generally Lisa Heinzerling, *The FDA's Plan B Fiasco: Lessons for Administrative Law*, 102 GEO. L.J. 927 (2014).

21 *Tummino*, 603 F. Supp. 2d at 535.

22 *See id.* at 549–50. After the judge remanded the matter back to the FDA, the FDA responded by making new determinations about the availability of Plan B. The task of defending those decisions fell to the Obama Administration. Yet the Obama Administration's FDA did not fare much better in the judge's eyes. *See* Tummino v. Hamburg, 936 F. Supp. 2d 162, 169–70 (E.D.N.Y. 2013) (finding that the FDA's handling of Plan B during the Obama Administration was "obviously political").

23 *See* ROBERT G. VAUGHN, THE SUCCESSES AND FAILURES OF WHISTLEBLOWER LAWS 72–85 (2012).

24 5 U.S.C. § 2302(b)(8)(A) (2012).

25 Dep't of Homeland Sec. v. MacLean, 135 S. Ct. 913 (2015).

26 Alan Maimon, *What Happens When a Whistleblower Returns to Work After a Decade's Fight*, WASH. POST (Mar. 3, 2016), https://goo.gl/zozmZT.

27 *See, e.g.*, Richard E. Moberly, *Unfulfilled Expectations: An Empirical Analysis of Why Sarbanes-Oxley Whistleblowers Rarely Win*, 49 WM. & MARY L. REV. 65, 67 (2007); *see also* Richard Moberly, *Sarbanes-Oxley's Whistleblower Provisions: Ten Years Later*, 64 S.C. L. REV. 1, 32–35 (2012).

CHAPTER 6

1 HARRY S. TRUMAN, TRUMAN SPEAKS 59 (1960).

2 *See, e.g.*, notes 4 & 5, *infra*.

3 By some accounts, federal courts only blocked two executive orders prior to Trump's entrance into office. *See, e.g.*, John C. Duncan, *A Critical Consideration of Executive Orders: Glimmerings of Autopoiesis in the Executive Role*, 35 VT. L. REV. 333, 337 (2010) (citing *Youngstown Sheet & Tube Co. v. Sawyer*, 343 U.S. 579 (1951), and *Chamber of Commerce v. Reich*, 74 F.3d 1322 (D.C. Cir. 1996)). Duncan's tally appears to exclude at least one executive order whose enjoinment was overturned on appeal. *See* Bldg. & Const. Trades Dep't, AFL-CIO v. Allbaugh, 172 F. Supp. 2d 138, 142 (D.D.C. 2001), *rev'd*, 295 F.3d 28 (D.C. Cir. 2002). It is important to recognize that the tallies identified here refer only to the enjoinment of executive orders issued by the president himself. They exclude agency rules and policies, which are much more frequently put on hold by the federal courts.

4 *See, e.g.*, Int'l Refugee Assistance Project v. Trump, 241 F. Supp. 3d 539 (D. Md.), *aff'd in part, vacated in part*, 857 F.3d 554 (4th Cir. 2017), *as amended* (May 31, 2017 & June 15, 2017), *vacated as moot*, No. 16-1436, 2017 WL 4518553 (U.S. Oct. 10, 2017) (mem.); Darweesh v. Trump, No. 17 Civ. 480 (AMD), 2017 WL 388504 (E.D.N.Y. Jan. 28, 2017); *see also* Washington v. Trump, No. C17-0141JLR, 2017 WL 462040 (W.D. Wash. Feb. 3, 2017).

5 County of Santa Clara v. Trump, 250 F. Supp. 3d 497 (N.D. Cal. 2017).

6 An exception was President William Henry Harrison, who died only a month into his term.

7 *See* Aaron Blake, *Trump Says 17-Month-Old Gay Marriage Ruling Is 'Settled' Law— but 43-Year-Old Abortion Ruling Isn't*, WASH. POST (Nov. 14, 2016), https://goo.gl/wrUSrN. *See also* Roe v. Wade, 410 U.S. 113 (1973); Obergefell v. Hodges, 135 S. Ct. 2584 (2015).

8 *But see* note 28 of chapter 2, *supra*.

9 Letter from John Jay et al., Justices, U.S. Supreme Court, to George Washington, President, United States (Aug. 8, 1793), https://perma.cc/2P5Z-AD5W.

10 *Id.*

11 Complaint for Declaratory Relief at 4, Smith v. Obama, 217 F. Supp. 3d 283 (D.D.C. 2016) (No. 16-843), https://perma.cc/NR3M-LW6Z.

12 *Id.* at 2.

13 *Smith*, 217 F. Supp. 3d at 297, https://perma.cc/BXJ5-VDVA.

14 Goldwater v. Carter, 444 U.S. 996, 1002–06 (1979) (Rehnquist, J., concurring in the judgment) (mem.).

15 *Id.* at 996.

16 Bush v. Gore, 531 U.S. 98 (2000).

17 Nat'l Fed'n of Indep. Bus. v. Sebelius, 567 U.S. 519, 537–38 (2012).

18 *Id.* at 538.

19 *Id.*

20 *Marbury v. Madison*, 5 U.S. 137 (1803).

21 *Id.* at 177.

22 *See* Printz v. United States, 521 U.S. 898 (1997).

23 *See* Shelby County v. Holder, 133 S. Ct. 2612 (2013).

24 *See* Boumediene v. Bush, 553 U.S. 723 (2008).

25 *See* United States v. Alvarez, 567 U.S. 709 (2012).

26 Cong. Research Serv., The Constitution of the United States of
    America: Analysis and Interpretation 2325–75 (Michael J. Garcia et al. eds.,
    2017), https://perma.cc/2DG7-8EFM.

27 Humphrey's Ex'r v. United States, 295 U.S. 602, 619 (1935).

28 Federal Trade Commission Act, Pub. L. 63-203, § 1, 38 Stat. 717, 718 (1914)
    (codified as amended at 15 U.S.C. § 41 (2012)); *see also Humphrey's Ex'r*, 295 U.S. at 619.

29 *Humphrey's Ex'r*, 295 U.S. at 631.

30 United States v. Nixon, 418 U.S. 683 (1974).

31 Christopher H. Schroeder, *The Story of* United States v. Nixon: *The President and
    the Tapes, in* Presidential Power Stories 327, 363 (Christopher H. Schroeder &
    Curtis A. Bradley eds., 2009).

32 Nixon v. Fitzgerald, 457 U.S. 731, 756 (1982). With respect to requests for injunctive
    relief, the law is more ambiguous. While the Supreme Court has not squarely held
    that plaintiffs are barred categorically from seeking injunctions against the president
    for official acts, it has indicated that, generally speaking, the federal courts have "no
    jurisdiction of a bill to enjoin the President in the performance of his official duties."
    Franklin v. Massachusetts, 505 U.S. 788, 802–803 (1992) (internal quotation marks
    omitted); *see also* Mississippi v. Johnson, 71 U.S. 475 (1867); Newdow v. Bush, 391
    F. Supp. 2d 95, 106 (D.D.C. 2005) ("[T]he Supreme Court has sent a clear message
    that an injunction should not be issued against the President for official acts."). As
    a result of these precedents, plaintiffs generally seek injunctions against executive
    branch officials and agencies rather than against the president in name.

33 Chevron, U.S.A., Inc. v. Nat. Res. Def. Council, Inc., 467 U.S. 837, 865–66 (1984).

34 *Id.*

35 *Id.* at 866.

36 *Id.* (internal quotation marks omitted).

37 Defining and Delimiting the Exemptions for Executive, Administrative,
    Professional, Outside Sales and Computer Employees, 81 Fed. Reg. 32,391
    (May 23, 2016) (to be codified at 29 C.F.R. pt. 541).

38 *See* Nevada v. U.S. Dep't of Labor, 218 F. Supp. 3d 520, 531 (E.D. Tex. 2016).

39 Motor Vehicle Mfrs. Ass'n v. State Farm Mut. Auto. Ins. Co., 463 U.S. 29, 59 (1983) (Rehnquist, J., concurring in part and dissenting in part).

40 *Id.*

41 *See, e.g.*, Eric Lipton, *Courts Thwart Administration's Effort to Rescind Obama-Era Environmental Regulations*, N.Y. Times (Oct. 6, 2017), https://goo.gl/9nqkqj.

42 Clinton v. Jones, 520 U.S. 681 (1997).

43 *Id.* at 697.

44 *Id.* at 702.

45 *Id.*

46 *See, e.g.*, Steve Vladeck & Benjamin Wittes, *Can a President's Absolute Immunity Be Trumped?*, Lawfare (May 9, 2017), https://perma.cc/64GV-VKSH.

47 Linda Greenhouse, *Justices, 5-4, Back Detainee Appeals for Guantánamo*, N.Y. Times (June 13, 2008), https://goo.gl/VhPpYD.

48 156 Cong. Rec. S266 (daily ed. Jan. 27, 2010) (President Obama's State of the Union).

49 Donald J. Trump (@realDonaldTrump), Twitter (Feb. 5, 2017, 12:39 PM), https://perma.cc/KVY6-NAS4.

50 Donald J. Trump (@realDonaldTrump), Twitter (Feb. 4, 2017, 5:12 AM), https://perma.cc/FV6D-KLWD.

51 Press Release, The White House, Statement on Sanctuary Cities Ruling (Apr. 25, 2017), https://perma.cc/Y537-2XQ5.

52 Washington v. Trump, 858 F.3d 1168, 1185 (9th Cir. 2017) (Bybee, J., dissenting) (mem.).

53 Donald J. Trump (@realDonaldTrump), Twitter (Feb. 9, 2017, 3:35 PM), https://perma.cc/H785-JA4S.

CHAPTER 7

1   Gregory v. Ashcroft, 501 U.S. 452, 458 (1991).

2   U.S. Term Limits, Inc. v. Thornton, 514 U.S. 779, 838 (1995) (Kennedy, J., concurring).

3   There are, of course, outer limits to the flexibility that states have vis-à-vis their own governments. To identify two prominent restrictions, state governments cannot violate the U.S. Constitution's prohibitions on establishing a religion or its protections of individuals' equal-protection rights. *See* U.S. Const. amend. I; *id.* amend. XIV, § 1. In addition, the Constitution provides that "[t]he United States shall guarantee to every State in this Union a Republican Form of Government." U.S. Const. art. IV, § 4, cl. 1. *But see* Luther v. Borden, 48 U.S. 1 (1849) (concluding that the federal courts lack the power to enforce this guarantee). Notwithstanding such restrictions, the Constitution permits the states wide latitude in designing and running their own governments.

4   U.S. CONST. art. VI, cl. 2 ("This Constitution, and the Laws of the United States which shall be made in Pursuance thereof; and all Treaties made, or which shall be made, under the Authority of the United States, shall be the supreme Law of the Land . . . .").

5   While the reach of Congress's legislative power is extremely broad, the Supreme Court has held that it is not unlimited. *See, e.g.,* United States v. Morrison, 529 U.S. 598 (2000) (holding that Congress lacked the power to enact parts of the Violence Against Women Act); United States v. Lopez, 514 U.S. 549 (1995) (holding that Congress lacked the power to enact a statute that criminally prohibited the mere possession of a firearm in a school zone).

6   E. ANN CARSON & ELIZABETH ANDERSON, BUREAU OF JUSTICE STATISTICS, U.S. DEP'T OF JUSTICE, NCJ 250229, PRISONERS IN 2015, at 3 tbl.1 (2016), http://perma.cc/N8XY-VLZK.

7   *See generally* Printz v. United States, 521 U.S. 898 (1997); New York v. United States, 505 U.S. 144 (1992).

8   *See* Garcia v. San Antonio Metro. Transit Auth., 469 U.S. 528, 530–31 (1985).

9   *See Printz,* 521 U.S. at 935.

10 This conclusion flows from the principles set forth in the Supreme Court's anticommandeering jurisprudence, which has been primarily focused on congressional attempts to commandeer via its Article I, Section 8 powers. It remains possible that the federal courts would, in some other circumstance, construe the Constitution as allowing commandeering of state governments or officers—for example, were Congress to attempt to commandeer via the authority it has under the Reconstruction Amendments or the Article I Elections Clause. However, even in that circumstance, it is difficult to imagine the federal courts concluding that the Constitution allows the federal government to compel states to make arrests on its behalf or otherwise engage in the types of commandeering discussed in chapter 7.

11 While an "expedited removal" process used by the federal government does cut back on some of this work, individuals subjected to this expedited process are still entitled to at least basic procedural protections prior to deportation.

12 Texas v. United States, 809 F.3d 134, 188 (5th Cir. 2015) (King, J., dissenting).

13 *See* Arizona v. United States, 567 U.S. 387 (2012).

14 Peter H. Schuck, *Taking Immigration Federalism Seriously,* 2007 U. CHI. LEGAL F. 57, 72 (2007).

15 *See New York,* 505 U.S. at 176 ("Either type of federal action would 'commandeer' state governments into the service of federal regulatory purposes, and would for this reason be inconsistent with the Constitution's division of authority between federal and state governments."). *See also* note 10, *supra* (describing possible caveats).

16 *See Printz,* 521 U.S. at 935. *See also* note 10, *supra* (describing possible caveats).

17 *See* Galarza v. Szalczyk, 745 F.3d 634, 643 (3d Cir. 2014) ("Under the Tenth
Amendment, immigration officials may not order state and local officials to
imprison suspected aliens subject to removal at the request of the federal government.
Essentially, the federal government cannot command the government agencies of
the states to imprison persons of interest to federal officials.").

18 *See, e.g.*, South Dakota v. Dole, 483 U.S. 203 (1987).

19 *See* note 10, *supra* (describing possible caveats).

20 *See generally* Arizona v. United States, 567 U.S. 387 (2012).

CHAPTER 8

1   GARFIELD'S WORDS: SUGGESTIVE PASSAGES FROM THE PUBLIC AND PRIVATE
WRITINGS OF JAMES ABRAM GARFIELD 143 (William Ralston Balch ed., 1881).

2   THE JEFFERSONIAN CYCLOPEDIA: A COMPREHENSIVE COLLECTION OF THE VIEWS
OF THOMAS JEFFERSON 803 (John P. Foley ed., 1900).

3   11 THE WRITINGS OF THOMAS JEFFERSON 224 (Albert Ellery Bergh ed., 1907).

4   CNN has compiled a number of its reports on a webpage titled "VA Hospital
Investigation," which is available at http://www.cnn.com/specials/us/va-hospitals.

5   U.S. CONST. amend. I ("Congress shall make no law ... abridging the freedom
of speech, or of the press ....").

6   *See generally* Obsidian Finance Group, LLC v. Cox, 740 F.3d 1284 (9th Cir. 2014).

7   *See* JEFFREY GOTTFRIED & ELISA SHEARER, PEW RESEARCH CTR., NEWS USE ACROSS
SOCIAL MEDIA PLATFORMS 2016 (2016), https://perma.cc/AR58-6MPX.

8   N.Y. Times Co. v. United States, 403 U.S. 713, 714 (1971) ("Any system of prior
restraints of expression comes to this Court bearing a heavy presumption against its
constitutional validity." (internal quotation marks and citation omitted)).

9   *Id.* at 715–16 (Black, J., concurring) (emphasis omitted).

10 N.Y. Times Co. v. Sullivan, 376 U.S. 254, 279–80 (1964).

11 Adam Liptak, *Can Trump Change Libel Laws?*, N.Y. Times (March 30, 2017),
https://goo.gl/5F8QMb.

12 *Id.*

13 In January 2017, President Obama commuted the bulk of Manning's sentence.
Obama had the legal power to take this step based on the authority to pardon that
the Constitution vests in the president. *See* U.S. CONST. art. II, § 2 ("The President
shall ... have Power to Grant Reprieves and Pardons for Offenses against the United
States, except in Cases of Impeachment."). Four months later, Manning was released
from prison.

14 *See, e.g.*, David Folkenflik, *Q: Could U.S. Prosecute Reporters for Classified Scoops?
A: Maybe*, NPR (Mar. 22, 2017), https://goo.gl/yGm5RL.

15   5 U.S.C. § 552 (2012 & Supp. 2016).

16   Ted Bridis, *Obama's Final Year: US Spent $36 Million in Records Lawsuits*, AP (Mar. 14, 2017), https://perma.cc/7KRD-ZBE3.

17   Letter from the American Civil Liberties Union to Melissa Golden, Lead Paralegal and FOIA Specialist (January 19, 2017), https://perma.cc/3WWW-YWS9.

18   *See, e.g.*, Tara John, *Donald Trump on North Korea: President Obama Should Have Taken Care of It*, TIME (Oct. 12, 2017), https://perma.cc/BA7Z-Z6WY; Donald J. Trump (@realDonaldTrump), TWITTER (Aug. 14, 2016, 5:37 AM), https://perma.cc/QP52-5RCC; Donald J. Trump (@realDonaldTrump), TWITTER (Feb. 15, 2017, 3:40 AM), https://perma.cc/5D4T-XXV4.

19   Donald J. Trump (@realDonaldTrump), TWITTER (Feb. 17, 2017, 1:48 PM), https://perma.cc/BC8T-C7L8.

20   *See, e.g.*, Emma Jane Kirby, *The City Getting Rich from Fake News*, BBC (Dec. 5, 2016), https://perma.cc/7JKA-KX5R.

21   *Transcript of the Democratic Presidential Debate*, N.Y. TIMES (Feb. 5, 2016), https://goo.gl/gxRFaA.

22   Niraj Chokshi, *Trump Accuses Clinton of Guiding Global Elite Against U.S. Working Class*, N.Y. TIMES (Oct. 13, 2016), https://goo.gl/c5moJi.

23   *See, e.g.*, Maggie McKinley, *Lobbying and the Petition Clause*, 68 STAN. L. REV. 1131 (2016) (describing—but challenging—the conventional legal wisdom, which is that the Constitution's Petition Clause protects the system of lobbying currently dominant in the United States).

24   Lee Hamilton, *What Makes a Strong Lobbyist*, IND. UNIV. CTR. ON REPRESENTATIVE GOV'T (Nov. 26, 2014), https://perma.cc/B5ZG-89KE.

25   *See, e.g.*, note 23, *supra*.

26   *See* FED. ELECTIONS COMM'N, OFFICIAL 2016 PRESIDENTIAL GENERAL ELECTION RESULTS (2017), https://perma.cc/AT2N-XKET.

27   *Id.*; *see also* Kiersten Schmidt & Wilson Andrews, *A Historic Number of Electors Defected, and Most Were Supposed to Vote for Clinton*, N.Y. TIMES (Dec. 19, 2016), https://goo.gl/zrZqBJ.

CHAPTER 9

1   Remarks at Georgetown University, 2017 DAILY COMP. PRES. DOC. 2 (June 25, 2017), https://perma.cc/G5HR-YDHS.

2   *See* Michael B. Gerrard, *Introduction and Overview, in* GLOBAL CLIMATE CHANGE AND U.S. LAW 3, 25 (Michael B. Gerrard & Jody Freeman eds., 2d ed. 2014).

3   Ryan Lizza, *As the World Burns*, NEW YORKER (Oct. 11, 2010), https://goo.gl/W1ZmNm.

4 Editorial Board, *Congress's Head-in-the-Sand Approach to Climate Change*, Wash. Post (July 6, 2014), https://goo.gl/K7yWpn.

5 42 U.S.C. § 7521(a)(1) (2012).

6 Control of Emissions from New Highway Vehicles and Engines, 68 Fed. Reg. 52,922 (Sept. 8, 2003).

7 Massachusetts v. EPA, 415 F.3d 50, 58 (D.C. Cir. 2005) (quoting Envtl. Def. Fund v. EPA, 598 F.2d 62, 82 (D.C. Cir. 1978)), *rev'd*, 549 U.S. 497 (2007).

8 *Id.* at 82 (Tatel, J., dissenting).

9 *Id.* at 60 (Sentelle, J., dissenting in part and concurring in the judgment).

10 *Massachusetts v. EPA*, 549 U.S. 497, 532 (2007).

11 *Id.* at 558–59 (Scalia, J., dissenting).

12 *See* Lisa Heinzerling, *Inside EPA: A Former Insider's Reflections on the Relationship Between the Obama EPA and the Obama White House*, 31 Pace Envtl. L. Rev. 325, 332, 336–37 (2014).

13 *See* Felicity Barringer, *White House Refused To Open Pollutants E-Mail*, N.Y. Times (June 25, 2008), https://goo.gl/rdzqWw.

14 Heidi Kitrosser, *Accountability and Administrative Structure*, 45 Willamette L. Rev. 607, 609 (2009).

15 42 U.S.C. § 7521(a)(1) (2012).

16 Endangerment and Cause or Contribute Findings for Greenhouse Gases Under Section 202(a) of the Clean Air Act, 74 Fed. Reg. 66,496 (Dec. 15, 2009), https://perma.cc/XCN2-RDWD.

17 Allie Malloy & Sunlen Serfaty, *Obama Unveils Major Climate Change Proposal*, CNN (Aug. 3, 2015), https://perma.cc/V6AS-Q66P.

18 *Id.*

19 Lucy Perkins & Bill Chappell, *President Obama Unveils New Power Plant Rules in 'Clean Power Plan,'* NPR (Aug. 3, 2015), https://goo.gl/5si1io.

20 *See* Order in Pending Case, West Virginia v. EPA, No. 15A773 (S. Ct. February 9, 2016), https://perma.cc/69DK-GFWR.

21 Exec. Order No. 13,783, 82 Fed. Reg. 16,093 (Mar. 31, 2017), https://perma.cc/FN58-PFQX.

22 Coral Davenport & Alissa J. Rubin, *Trump Signs Executive Order Unwinding Obama Climate Policies*, N.Y. Times (Mar. 28, 2017), https://goo.gl/HpXQHy.

23 Juliet Eilperin & Brady Dennis, *Court Freezes Clean Power Plan Lawsuit, Signaling Likely End to Obama's Signature Climate Policy*, Wash. Post (Apr. 28, 2017), https://goo.gl/qZyroJ.

24 *See, e.g.*, Donald J. Trump (@realDonaldTrump), Twitter (Dec. 6, 2013, 7:38 AM), https://perma.cc/3ZQW-ZMZQ.

25 Donald J. Trump (@realDonaldTrump), Twitter (Nov. 6, 2012, 11:15 AM), https://perma.cc/Q6PA-FJJ9.

26 Brent Kendall & Amy Harder, *Obama Power-Plant Emissions Rule Faces Key Test in Court*, Wall St. J. (Sept. 25, 2016), https://goo.gl/eMQ12x.

27 Remarks Announcing United States Withdrawal from the United Nations Framework Convention on Climate Change Paris Agreement, 2017 Daily Comp. Pres. Doc. 1–2 (June 1, 2017), https://perma.cc/BW79-P8DM.

28 News Release, EPA, EPA Takes Another Step to Advance President Trump's America First Strategy, Proposes Repeal of "Clean Power Plan" (Oct. 10, 2017), https://perma.cc/2UJL-KED4.

29 42 U.S.C. § 7543(e)(2) (2012).

30 *See* U.S. Climate Alliance, https://www.usclimatealliance.org/.

31 Juliana v. United States, 217 F. Supp. 3d 1224, 1234 (D. Or. 2016).

32 *Id.* at 1243.

33 *Id.* at 1236 (citing U.S. Dep't of Commerce v. Montana, 503 U.S. 442, 458 (1992)).

34 *Id.* at 1263.

35 *Id.* at 1243.

CHAPTER 10

1 *Inaugural Address, 20 January 1961*, John F. Kennedy Presidential Libr. & Museum (Jan. 20, 1961), https://perma.cc/BXM3-ZPGJ.

2 *See Tips for Submitting Effective Comments*, Regulations.gov, https://perma.cc/E8AC-PP36; *What Is Effective Commenting?*, RegulationRoom, https://perma.cc/9N2B-3PZC; Envtl. Law Inst., Ocean Program, Public Participation in Environmental Decision-Making: Step-By-Step Tips for Writing Effective Public Comments (2013), https://perma.cc/G8UM-DE9P.

3 *See How To File a Petition for Rulemaking*, Ctr. for Effective Gov't, https://perma.cc/8MXJ-MV4G.

4 *See Our Story*, iCivics, https://goo.gl/w7EwJ4.

Acknowledgments

We are indebted to the many colleagues, editors, and friends who have provided invaluable assistance on this project. At the outset, we thank the lawyers and legal academics who have brought their expertise to bear. This group includes Angélica Cházaro, MJ Durkee, Bob Gomulkiewicz, Brianne Gorod, Sanne Knudsen, Nick Manheim, Sarah Nicholson, Liz Porter, Lauren Sancken, Sallie Sanford, Hugh Spitzer, Kellye Testy, Thomas Tongue, Tom Tongue, Steve Vladeck, Todd Wildermuth, and David Ziff. We are similarly grateful to those who have provided insight from a nonlegal perspective, including Steffenie Evans, Charles Lobitz, Gretchen Lobitz, Vivienne Manheim, Andrea Tongue, and Andrew Watts. Gratitude is also due to our editors and designers, including Dan Crissman, Cynthia Fester, Rachel Fudge, David Provolo, and Susannah Noel, as well as to our student assistants, including Alex Arkfeld, Ben Crozier, Marten King, Jason Parfet, and Maricarmen Perez-Vargas. Finally, we are grateful for the assistance of the outstanding librarians at the Gallagher Law Library at the University of Washington School of Law, for the generous financial support provided by the University of Washington School of Law, and for research funds dedicated to the Jack R. MacDonald Endowed Chair.

About the Authors

Lisa Marshall Manheim is a lawyer and associate professor of law at the University of Washington School of Law. After graduating from Yale Law School, Professor Manheim worked as a law clerk for two federal judges, Justice Anthony M. Kennedy of the U.S. Supreme Court and Judge Pierre N. Leval of the U.S. Court of Appeals for the Second Circuit. She then worked at the law firm Perkins Coie LLP, where she specialized in appellate practice, commercial litigation, and political law. Professor Manheim teaches courses in constitutional law, election law, and the federal courts, and she has won awards for her teaching. Her research explores constitutional decision-making, election-related litigation, and judicial review of presidential actions. She has published her work in leading academic journals, as well as popular publications such as the *New York Times*.

Kathryn Watts is a lawyer and professor of law at the University of Washington School of Law, where she holds the Jack R. MacDonald Endowed Chair. After graduating from Northwestern University School of Law, Professor Watts worked as a law clerk for two federal judges, Justice John Paul Stevens of the U.S. Supreme Court and Judge A. Raymond Randolph of the U.S. Court of Appeals for the D.C. Circuit. She then worked at the law firm Sidley Austin LLP. Professor Watts teaches courses in administrative law, constitutional law, and Supreme Court decision-making. Professor Watts's research explores, among other topics, presidential control over the regulatory state and the interaction between federal courts and agencies. She has published her work in top academic journals such as the *Yale Law Journal* and the *Harvard Law Review*, and she is a coauthor of *The Supreme Court Sourcebook*. She has received awards for her teaching and scholarship.

Follow us on Twitter! We are @ManheimAndWatts.

Made in the USA
Middletown, DE
18 January 2018